Productivity
and Quality Improvement

IFS

Productivity and Quality Improvement

Johnson Aimie Edosomwan

IFS (Publications) Ltd, UK
Springer-Verlag
Berlin · Heidelberg · New York · Tokyo
1988

Johnson Aimie Edosomwan
IBM (AG) Headquarters
Mount Pleasant
New York 10591
USA

British Library Cataloguing in Publication Data

Edosomwan, Johnson.
  Productivity and quality improvement.
  1. Productivity. Improvement. Manuals.
  2. Manufacturing industries. Quality
  control. Manuals
I. Title
658.3'14

ISBN 1-85423-002-6

ISBN 1-85423-002-6 IFS Publications
ISBN 3-540-50452-4 Springer-Verlag Berlin Heidelberg New York Tokyo
ISBN 0-387-50452-4 Springer-Verlag New York Heidelberg Berlin Tokyo

© 1988 IFS Ltd, 35–39 High Street, Kempston, Bedford MK42 7BT, UK
and Springer-Verlag Berlin Heidelberg New York Tokyo.

Phototypeset by Area Graphics Ltd, Letchworth, UK.

Printed and bound by Short Run Press Ltd, Exeter, UK.

CONTENTS

ACKNOWLEDGEMENTS

Many people contributed to the completion of this book. My thanks to Mrs Isiwatu Badiru and Joelle Stufano who helped on many occasions during the preparation of this book. My appreciation and love is expressed to my wife and children for their support and encouragement. I am also grateful to my teachers: John W. Kendrick, Edwards W. Deming, David J. Sumanth, Carl M. Kromp, Seymour Melman, Robert C. Karasek, Tarek M. Khalil, James N. Mosel, and Robert C. Waters for providing the right training. My thanks to my employer, IBM, for the support and encouragement. I am also grateful for the guidance received from God during the preparation of this book.

INTRODUCTION:
WHY THIS GUIDE WAS WRITTEN

This guide was written because of several requests by industrial managers, engineers, consultants and students over the past decade. The feedback that I received from practising and teaching productivity and quality management indicated that a practical and pragmatic approach to resolving productivity and quality problems is required in the modern business environment. I have experienced numerous successes in using some basic, down-to-earth approaches and techniques in improving productivity and quality in both the manufacturing and service industry sectors. The requests from my various clients (industrial managers, students and other practitioners) encouraged me to present my ideas on productivity and quality improvement at the source in a simple, short, practical guide that is easy to use

This guide was written with the belief that achieving productivity and quality improvement at the source does not require sophisticated knowledge of statistics and productivity formulae. What is required is commitment from both management and employees to do the job right the first time, at the source, through the application of basic skills, tools and techniques. This guide is also based on the premise that an integrated systems approach to problem solving can lead to effective resolution of problems and barriers that hinder productivity and quality improvement.

Productivity and quality improvement at the source does not happen by accident. It requires organised use of common sense and an integrated process, involving both management and employees with the ultimate goal of managing the design, development, production, transfer and use of the various types of products or services in both the work environment and market-place. Productivity and quality improvement require on-going commitment from everyone to excellence in the management of business processes, product and services.

This guide was written also to satisfy the need that exists on how to manage the production and service process, respond to customer demand effectively and be profitable in a competitive world economy.

What this guide attempts to accomplish

This guide is meant to provide specific techniques, tools, methodologies and principles for improving productivity and quality at the source of production or service. The guide focuses on how to apply productivity and quality tools and techniques at the source to provide the final product or service to the customer defect-free. It is organised into five sections. Section one describes the requirements and principles for improving productivity and quality at the source. The definitions of productivity and quality technologies are offered as well as an effective management system for productivity and quality improvement. In Section two, specific just-in-time quality assessment and improvement tools are presented. This section focuses on statistical process control, the construction and use of histogram, Pareto diagram, cause and effect diagram, matrix analysis technique, quality error removal technique, and the design of experiments for problem resolution at the source. Section three focuses on productivity mechanisms for eliminating bottle-necks and barriers that hinder productivity improvement effort. A framework for problem solving is offered as well as process management techniques, performance improvement techniques, and productivity assessment and improvement tools. In Section four, specific frameworks, methodologies and techniques are offered for managing the connection and relationship between productivity and quality. The cost of quality is examined. The models for productivity and quality assessment and management are also presented. Guidelines for implementing productivity and quality improvement projects are presented in Section five. This section also focuses on the common sources of failure as well as strategies for overcoming common problems. The appendices present productivity and quality management exercises for a training workshop on the subject. The instruments for implementing productivity and quality improvement techniques at the source are also provided. Productivity and statistical formulae and tables, glossary of terms and extensive bibliography are offered.

The guide is based on tools, techniques, and methodologies that have been tested in real life situations. It also reflects over a decade of practical experience in actually developing and implementing specific programmes to improve productivity and quality at the company level.

To whom this guide is addressed

This practical guide is meant to help industrial managers, decision makers, consultants, workers and students in having a quick source of reference for productivity and quality improvements techniques, tools, methodologies, and principles for achieving defect-free output at the source of production or service.

How to use this guide

This guide has been presented in a logical step-by-step approach in both narrative materials and flow diagrams. Specific examples are provided where required to illustrate how specific tools and techniques are used. The Productivity and Quality Improvement Matrix (PAQIT) presented in Table 1 is provided to assist the user of this guide to decide which tool or techniques to select in a given situation. The following steps are recommended for using this guide:

- **Step one:** Read the entire guide to understand the concepts and flow of material presented. Use PAQIT presented in Table 1 to understand the benefits and applicable areas of the tools presented.
- **Step two:** Read the specific section of interest thoroughly to understand how the tools and techniques in that section can be used to improve productivity and quality at the source. Read supplemental materials on the same subject as required. It is assumed that this guide will be augmented by both industrial work experience and more theoretically complete academic experience on productivity and quality management where necessary.
- **Step three:** Go through the self-assessment example using the tools and concept learned from step two.
- **Step four:** Implement the knowledge acquired to improve productivity and quality at the source in your organisation. The best way to test the validity of the tools provided is through implementation and follow-up on corrective actions.

How to begin the continuous improvement task

Recognise the following productivity and quality improvement concepts and guidelines:

- Productivity and quality improvement result from continuous improvement action from both management and employees.

Table 1 Productivity and quality improvement tools (PAQIT)

Principles / Techniques	Applications area				Potential benefits							
Conceptual frameworks / Methodologies / Tools	Individual/task level	Customer supplier and producer levels	Project and programme management	Team-work and technical departments	Problem analysis and identification	Process improvement	Measurement and evaluation of process	Adequate planning	Enhancing teamwork	Improving team communication	Eliminating team barriers/bottlenecks	Roles/responsibility definition
Twelve productivity and quality management principles	X	X	X	X	X	X	X	X	X	X	X	X
6C principles	X		X	X					X	X	X	X
PAQAM	X	X	X	X	X	X	X	X	X		X	X
PAQMM	X	X	X	X	X	X	X	X	X	X	X	X
Hypothesis testing	X	X		X	X	X	X					
Statistical process control	X	X	X	X	X	X	X	X	X	X	X	X
Nominal group technique		X	X	X		X		X	X	X	X	X
Just-in-time technique	X	X	X	X	X		X	X	X	X	X	
Design of experiment	X	X	X	X	X	X	X			X		

Technique													
Matrix analysis technique	X	X	X	X	X	X		X			X	X	X
Pareto diagram	X	X	X	X	X	X					X		X
Cause-and-effect diagram	X	X	X	X									
Method analysis technique	X	X	X	X	X	X		X	X	X	X	X	X
Value analysis approach	X	X	X	X	X								
Scatter diagram	X	X		X	X		X	X				X	X
TOTPM	X	X		X	X		X					X	X
Productivity measurement													
Control charts	X	X	X	X	X	X	X	X	X	X	X	X	X
Process management technique	X	X	X	X	X	X	X	X	X	X		X	X
Equal productivity curve	X	X	X	X	X		X						
Cost curve	X	X	X	X	X	X	X	X	X	X	X	X	X
PASIT/Task specification	X	X	X	X	X	X		X	X	X	X	X	X
GPSF/QER	X	X	X	X	X	X	X	X	X	X	X	X	X
Inspection technique	X	X	X	X	X	X		X	X	X	X	X	X

- The company, functional units, departments, work groups and individuals have clearly defined goals and objectives. The mission of each operational units and individual should be defined without ambiguity.
- Everyone must be involved in the continuous improvement effort. Encourage teamwork and participative management style.
- Focus for improvement must be on every task, process, procedure, policy for each unit and must involve accountability by everyone.
- Create the right awareness that no level of defect is acceptable
- Provide people with access to the required information tools and techniques to do the job right.
- Focus on using basic, simple, effective tools.
- Obtain commitment from everyone to cost reduction and competitiveness through productivity and quality improvement.
- Leaders and managers should demonstrate commitment by example.
- Provide the right education and training.
- Begin by obtaining management and employee commitment to a specific pilot improvement project.
- Establish the right work plans and implement a pilot project with adequate productivity and quality tools.
- Measure the results obtained and take corrective action immediately.
- Sell the benefits obtained and build on demonstrated accomplishments and results.
- Continually encourage everyone to create the right vision of the improved process and operational unit.

1 PRODUCTIVITY AND QUALITY DEFINITIONS AND PRINCIPLES

Productivity and quality definitions

Productivity and quality technologies

Productivity and quality technologies are terms used to mean methods, techniques, tools and measurements that help in the planning, development, design, control, evaluation, management and improvement of the quality of products and services, and the productivity of each operational unit involved. When used correctly, productivity and quality technologies become a means of:

- Identifying critical processes that control the performance of the final product or service provided by each operational unit.
- Providing the assurance required for the manufacturing and service to specifications.
- Protecting the customer or consumer through delivery of defect-free product.

- Protecting the producer through adequate process control that eliminates defect and build quality into the product or service.
- Producing an essential source for both management and workers to solve daily production and service problems that affect the level of quality and productivity.
- Protecting the producer through achieving an understanding of the quality levels of incoming sub-assemblies, parts, materials and finished units.
- Establishing appropriate statistical process control limits for understanding when a particular process is out of control so that the appropriate problem can be analysed and resolved.
- Doing the job right at the source of production or service.

Productivity and quality technologies help us to manage the total requirement of a production or service system that has the degree of complexity specified in Fig. 1.1. In both the manufacturing and service work environments, productivity and quality technologies are required for the optimisation of input, process and output. The use of these technologies ensures that the problems and challenges affecting the level of productivity growth and quality improvement are addressed.

Productivity

Productivity is a measure of how well resources are utilised to produce output (goods and services). It relates output to input and also integrates performance aspects of quality, efficiency and effectiveness. The three types of productivity measures commonly used at the company level are:

- Total productivity is *the ratio of total output to all input factors.*
- Total factor productivity is *the ratio of total output to the sum of associated labour and capital (factor) inputs.*
- Partial productivity is *the ratio of total output to one class of input.*

The definition of productivity should not be confused with efficiency and effectiveness. Effectiveness is a measure of the outcome or output of an operational unit. It is a measure of how well an operational unit was able to accomplish its objective. Efficiency is a measure of the degree to which an operational unit utilises appropriate resources in the right manner.

Quality of management

The quality of management pertains to how well managers of operational units are best able to perform effectively the tasks of planning, organising, controlling, delegating and directing employees to produce goods and services of highest quality and deliver them, at the right time, at a competitive price. It also pertains to how well managers are able to motivate people

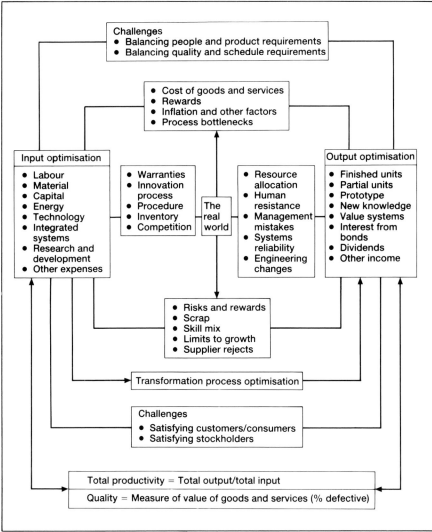

Fig. 1.1 Elements involved in managing the total requirements of production and service systems.

to do their best, to provide a good working environment and tools and to reward accomplishments. Excellent quality of management can be achieved through attention and through actions that address both people- and product-orientated issues.

Quality of goods and services

Quality is a measure of the value of goods and services as perceived by the supplier, producer and consumer. The measure also pertains to the degree to which products and services conform to specifications, requirements and standards at an acceptable price. The quality of work as it relates to both internal and external customers can be defined as the measure of how well a particular work output meets the requirements of the customer. In both the production and service work environments, quality of work pertains to the end-product or service and the quality of all transformation processes, and inputs used to provide the final goods and services.

When dealing with product quality, there are two other aspects of quality: the quality of design and the quality of conformance. Quality of design pertains to quality obtained through changes or manipulation in designing parameters. The differences in quality are a result of differences in size, materials used, tolerances in manufacturing, reliability, equipment utilised, and temperature. Quality of conformance is a measure of how well the product conforms to the specifications and tolerances required by the design. Such factors as training, the production process, motivation levels, procedures, and quality assurance systems can have an effect on the quality conformance.

Quality characteristics may be of several types:

- Time–oriented (serviceability, reliability, maintainability).
- Sensory (colour, taste, beauty, appearance, and others).
- Structural (including frequency, weight, length, and viscosity).
- Commercial (warranty).
- Behavioural or ethical (fairness, honesty, courtesy, and so on).

Productivity and quality management defined

Productivity and quality management form an integrated process involving both management and employees with the ultimate goal of managing the design, development, production, transfer, and use of the various types of products or services in both the work environment and the market-place. The process requires the total involvement of everyone in the planning, measurement, evaluation, control, and improvement of productivity and quality at the source of production or at the service centre.

Productivity and quality focus items and sources of errors

The common problems and sources of errors in productivity and quality management are presented in Figs. 1.2 and 1.3 respectively. The problems include those of convincing top management to support productivity and quality improvement programmes, projects and efforts; designing and justifying productivity and quality programme/process improvement process including the selection and application of the appropriate process management tools and techniques; developing appropriate implementation strategies for productivity and quality improvement projects. These strategies should address how to obtain the total involvement of both management and employee, minimisation of resistance to change attitude and follow-up actions on improvement projects.

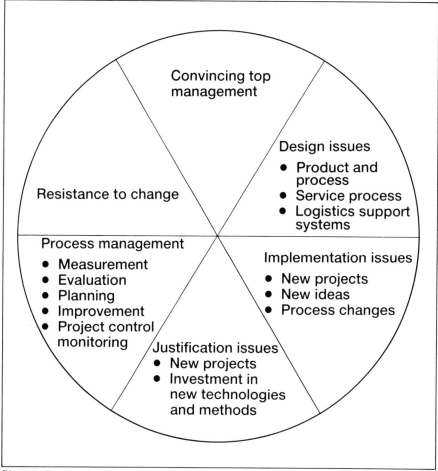

Fig. 1.2 Common problems in productivity and quality management.

Eighty per cent of productivity and quality errors are caused by management mistakes, especially in making inappropriate decisions on resource allocation, investment, the management of people and operational unit priorities. On the other hand, employees and workers, vendors, suppliers, and process related errors account for about 20% of errors. These sources of error are consistent in both manufacturing and service work environments.

The source of variation in a production or service process can be found in one or more of six areas. These are human induced errors, the methods and techniques, the materials, the environment, the machines (equipment and tools), and sudden changes in operating policies and procedures. Process-inherent sources of variation are built in as part of the process and are very difficult to eradicate. Variation due to assignable causes such as changes in product specification, tools and methods are easily corrected. However, assignable causes distort the process stability and distribution and if not corrected cause a given process to be out of control. Not all sources of errors

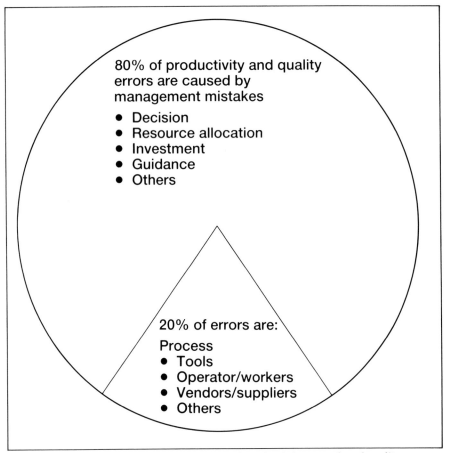

Fig. 1.3 Sources of errors that affect the level of productivity growth and quality improvement.

can be measured. Variation in products and processes can be measured. Variation caused by erratic changes in policy may be difficult to measure.

Essentials of productivity and quality improvement at the source of production or service

Achieving excellent and acceptable levels of output with high quality at the source of production and service requires careful attention to the following details:

Adequate work climate and teamwork

Productivity and quality improvement at the source is possible if the work environment is conducive to innovation and individual creativity, is hazard-free, and has the essential tools and techniques to assist both management and employees to perform given set of tasks correctly the first time. Total teamwork between management and employees, unions and other functional areas of the organisation is also essential. The teamwork approach should focus on eliminating the barriers that hinder improvement in productivity and quality. Everyone within the organisation must work towards a common goal – delivering the right product or service to the customer at minimum cost and excellent quality. Teamwork is usually highly achievable if there is a good working relationship between management, unions and employees. The relationship that exists between a manager and his employees is a key element in productivity and quality improvement. That relationship is the basis for positive or negative attitudes at work that have a direct bearing on output, quality and profitability. Both management and employees must work together and accept human behaviour as they are, and must seek better ways to enhance communication and teamwork. The key is to identify the personnel issues and shortcomings affecting performance and to do something about them. Continuous improvement effort should be applied to remove barriers and friction among individuals and work group. People should be trained to work together toward common goals and objectives while sharing ownership for the final output and results. Participative management style also encourages teamwork and innovation. An environment where employees and managers are able to participate in problem solving, decision making, process changes and planning improved performance provides fertile ground for improvement in productivity and quality.

The right training

Strong commitment and provision of the required tools, techniques and training can go a long way to improving productivity and quality at the source. The commitment to training should focus on items such as measurement tools, planning tools, evaluation tools, improvement tools, feedback mechanism, resource allocation, information systems, decision-making process, cultural support systems, performance balance and process control techniques. Training is essential because it prepares everyone to do his job well, by building the right knowledge that makes for logical, intelligent actions and decisions. If the right skills are provided for people, they attain efficient work habits and positive attitudes that promote co-operation and teamwork. Five approaches are recommended for training:

- Provide formal education.
- Provide on-the-job training through telling and directing process.
- Train the trainers – usually this reduces training costs.
- Explain the work processes through media such as video tapes.
- Provide group training and cross training on specific tasks.

The manager can play a key role in ensuring that the right training is provided for employees by allocating the right funds. An allocation scheme for training funds with specific recommended training programmes for management and employees is provided in Table 1.1 and Fig. 1.4 respectively. The training suggested in Table 1.1 is based on the assumption that both management and workers have already attained a formal acceptable level of education in productivity and quality management. Employees and managers who would improve productivity and quality must be selected with extreme care and trained thoroughly in the right methods, techniques and attitude for doing the job right. The truculent, ignorant, untrainable, and psychologically disturbed should never be allowed to supervise the work of the other people, yet many organisations select supervisors by the most random methods, train them not at all and wonder why productivity and quality do not evolve. Both management and employees should have at least 50 hours of training every year on new methods, techniques and enhancement in managerial skills. In addition to the training suggested in Table 1.1 the following training is suggested for managers: fundamentals of directing, planning, staffing, and controlling the work of people and projects; morale improvement techniques, salary and benefit administration; and how to handle grievances and facilitate teamwork.

Table 1.1 Recommended enhancement productivity and quality training programme for management and employees

Level	Training highlights	Training time required
Upper management	Productivity management principles Customer partnership Customer requirements Goal setting process Key service quality programmes Employee development programmes	One week initial training followed by 3 hours periodic training
Middle management	Resource allocation Programme development Programme maintenance Customer partnership Productivity management Quality management	1½ weeks initial training followed by 5 hours periodic training
Supervisors and first line managers	Programme maintenance Tools and techniques for managing quality programme Feedback mechanisms Productivity and quality management techniques	2 weeks initial training followed by 1 day periodic training
Technical personnel and workers	Tools for measurement control, planning and improvement Tools for reliability, assurance, durability and customer satisfaction Productivity and quality management techniques	3 weeks initial training followed by 2 days periodic training

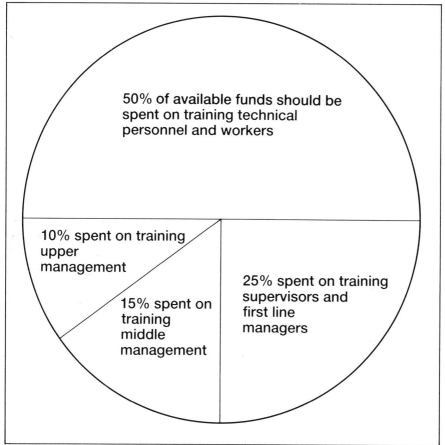

Fig. 1.4 Suggested allocation scheme for productivity and quality improvement training funds.

A balanced emphasis on people and product management

Often the pressure to produce more to satisfy customer orders leads managers to focus on product management issues only. This style can lead to neglect of employee development, degradation in the morale of employees and breakdown in communication within the organisation. Productivity and quality improvement require focus on people and product requirements. The manager's role in the improvement process is to provide the right level of encouragement, training, guidance, support and help as required. Usually, if the employees are properly supported, they will produce the right product and satisfy the customer orders. On the other hand, employees also have very important roles to play in ensuring that there is the mutual trust and confidence required to deliver the final output successfully. Employees who demonstrate strong ability, willingness to work, commitment to excellence and the right drive to achieve are what organisations are looking for. Both management and employees must accept responsibility for results and actions. The degree to which management and employees can be effective in improving productivity and quality depends on how well both can work together.

Adequate focus on providing the fundamentals for achieving excellence in products and service offerings

Organisations or operation units that have in place the right fundamentals for product and service management are bound to be successful in improving productivity and quality at all levels and sectors of work processes. The fundamentals of productivity and quality excellence are the corner stones of process and programme enhancement that lead to breakthrough in productivity and quality achievements. The recommended fundamentals for management and employee focus are presented in Fig. 1.5. Again, teamwork is essential to successful implementation of the recommended productivity and quality fundamentals. The strategies for productivity and quality improvement should also include: continually applying new ideas, technologies and techniques to improve new and existing product; involving people effectively in productivity and quality improvement initiatives, and practising participative management style through effective training to provide an excellent working relationship between suppliers, process owners, and customers.

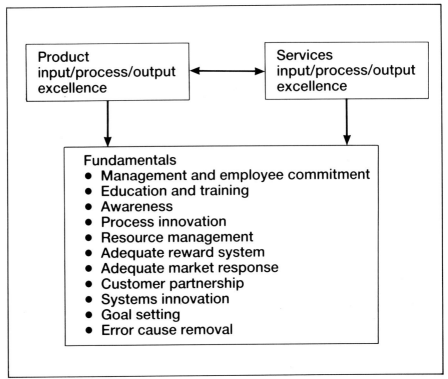

Fig. 1.5 Fundamentals for achieving excellence in product and service offerings.

Adequate focus on enhancing supplier task boundary

Productivity and quality errors can be minimised if there is an adequate mechanism in place to enhance the input quality from the suppliers. The timing and quality level of inputs provided by a supplier can make a difference in the level of productivity and quality obtained at the source in the receiving organisations. Fig. 1.6 presents the key elements that should be managed continuously to enhance supplier task boundary requirements.

Adequate focus on enhancing the relationship between process owner(s) and customer(s)

The services of both the internal and external customers are crucial to the success of any business unit. Productivity and quality service errors can best be understood if the following actions are in place to enhance customer input and partnership:

- On-line communication channel between process owner(s) and customer(s).
- Periodic survey conducted to access the degree of customer satisfaction regarding products and services offered.
- Customer participation in new products and services strategies.
- Feedback mechanism to customer(s) on improvements achieved in the production, delivery and consumption processes.
- Encouragement to suppliers to participate in productivity and quality programme implementation.
- Feedback from the customer on product and service pricing policy.

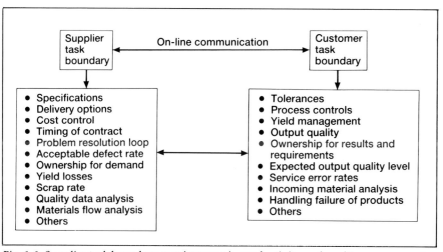

Fig. 1.6 Supplier task boundary requirements in productivity and quality management.

The process owner's first priority should be to satisfy the requirements of the customer. Unrealistic expectations from the customer can usually be resolved through good communication channels and practice, and through appropriate feedback mechanisms in place to monitor product and service performances.

Additional areas for enhancing process owner and customer/ partnership that require focus are presented in Fig. 1.7. Adequate customer partnership comes from management and employee willingness to take responsibility for results, to be accountable for all actions and to have the desire to provide assurance to satisfy the customer requirements. Several meetings between process owner(s) and customer(s) on product and services are recommended. Such meetings enhance overall business relationships, product development strategy and the expected quality of output.

Creation of awareness among management and employees that everyone has a customer

The notion that product or service quality is only important to the final customer outside the organisation should be discouraged. The right awareness to accept is that everyone within an organisation has both internal and external customers. Each individual customer of his or her own product or service is in turn the customer of people working in different tasks in various departments and operation units. Increasing productivity and reducing quality errors at the individual level of operation also ensures that excellent quality products and services are delivered to the ultimate customer.

Creation of the right awareness about the need for adequate measures and data

In order to control the production, service, delivery and consumption processes involved in producing products and services, adequate measures for both tangible and intangible elements are needed.

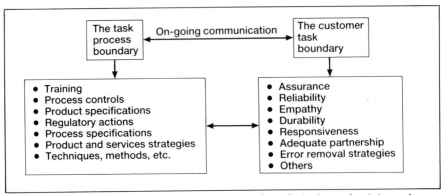

Fig. 1.7 Essentials of the task process and customer boundaries in productivity and quality management.

In the next section of this guide (Section two), tools for productivity and quality improvement are discussed. The essential element is that everyone within the organisation is trained on how to use the various measures for control, improvement, and planning. For measures to be meaningful and useful, there is the need to collect accurate data which truly represent the current state of the service process. Appropriate productivity and quality management data are also required to enable individuals to assess their own work, to control and correct errors at the source of production and service. Examples of the types of productivity and quality data used in a typical computer manufacturing environment are presented in Table 1.2.

Adequate procedures and controls for managing organisation and cross-functional task boundaries

Productivity and quality management also requires on-going attention to the bottle-necks in the organisation and to cross-functional process boundaries. Fig. 1.8 presents the key elements that must be addressed. It is

Table 1.2 Examples of productivity and quality data

Type of data	Source
System in-house performance data	Manufacturing engineering and quality assurance departments
System field performance data	Customer service departments Marketing representative sales data
Field replacement due to failure in service	Spare parts sales log Marketing representative sales data
Competitive quality ratings	A typical reliability plus: a quality report that evaluates systems reliability by sector and business area
Engineering changes updates	Manufacturing engineering and development quality reports
Service error rates implant	Individual control charts and system control charts
Field service error rates	System performance control charts at the customer
Productivity values and indexes	Manufacturing engineering and cost accounting
Workload levels	Industrial engineering, finance and controls
Productivity and financial forecasts	Business planning, finance and marketing departments

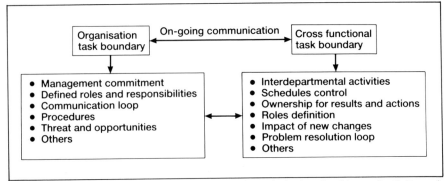

Fig. 1.8 Organisation and cross-functional task boundaries involved in productivity and quality management.

important for every business unit constantly to assess the ways in which business is conducted, and to make changes as required. The key is to identify the organisation's weaknesses and do something about them, while capitalising on the strengths.

Adequate focus on managing the total system requirements

Productivity and quality improvement at the source cannot be achieved through piecemeal ideas, actions and control. Excellent productivity and quality results are obtainable through focusing on managing the total requirements of each operational unit, supplier, customer, task, individual, department and the total organisation. Managing the total requirements involves the use of common sense and adequate technical and managerial skills to provide the right sense of direction for the business, supervising at the right level, with emphasis on approach training, counselling, coaching, training and performance feedback; providing the right level of positive reinforcement, motivation, recognition and encouragement; defining responsibilities adequately, and providing the authority, reward, punishment and accountability that go with each job. Management has a key role to play in managing the total requirements of the system. Appropriate management actions are required in the many areas, including:

- The authorisation and use of resources.
- Providing the link for timely response to problems and issues at the source of production or service.
- Ensuring that self-assessment is conducted at all levels.
- Creating the right awareness, training and education and leadership by example.
- Closing open problems and resolving issues quickly.
- Assigning the right ownership for responsibilities.
- Accepting the risk and reward involved in making difficult production and service management decisions.

Management of improvement requires focusing on the right company objectives, long-range planning, progress reviews, functional strategies, policy, procedures, controls, measurement and evaluation, and recognition for individual and group accomplishments. Appropriate supervisory actions that provide leadership by example, communicate concerns and the need for improvement to employees quickly, allow participation in decision-making and use organised programmes, can facilitate improvement in productivity and quality.

Total commitment from both management and employees to excellence through high quality and increased productivity provides a strong foundation. Individual abilities and drive to achieve excellence through quality of work are also strong attributes that are highly desirable.

Recommended principles for productivity and quality management

Principle one: The approach *to improving the process requires that management takes a leadership role in creating the right awareness and prioritising resources to the various improvement projects.*

Principle two: The theme *that should be communicated to everyone in the organisation is* continuous improvement is needed in the process.

Principle three: The scope *of the improvement effort should include all activities and tasks performed in the organisation.*

Principle four: The scale *of the improvement activities should specify that everyone is responsible.*

Principle five: The training *provided should include, but not be limited to, problem-solving techniques, decision-making techniques at the source of production or service, statistical process control, productivity and quality measurement, evaluation and improvement techniques, customer requirements management; planning tools, and project management.*

Principle six: The style *should focus on prevention system for defects and process bottle-necks. Inspection and non-value-adding operations used for detecting defects should be discouraged.*

Principle seven: The awareness *for everyone should focus on a vision of the improved process, excellent quality product and service.*

Principle eight: The method(s) *employed should be based on demonstrated results in providing adequate process yield and output.*

Principle nine: The standard *set should be that everyone does the job right the first time at the source.*

Principle ten: The measures *used for productivity and quality should include, but not be limited to, the following: partial, total factor and total productivities; per centage defective, customer satisfaction indexes, cost of quality, error rate indexes, process failure rate, and line control indexes.*

Principle eleven: The rewards and recognition *for improvement in productivity and quality should be given to both management and employees. Reward continuous improvement in a timely manner.*

Principle twelve: Teamwork *approach, of all functional areas, and* participative management style *should be encouraged. Focus on providing effective cultural support systems, consensus building, adequate mechanisms for recognising team performance.*

General approaches to productivity and quality improvement

Each organisation or enterprise unit has its own unique productivity and quality problems. The choice of which approach is likely to be successful depends on the type of problem to be resolved and the prevailing circumstances within the organisation under analysis. The approaches described in the following sections are recommended.

Work simplification and operations improvement

On-going analysis, review and study of the method of doing work within an operational unit must be performed, with the view of making the process simpler, the job easier, more nearly perfect, the workers smarter and more productive. These factors can be termed work simplifications:

- Work simplification is the systematic investigation and analysis of contemplated and present work systems and methods for the purpose of developing easier, quicker, less fatiguing, and more economical ways of providing high-quality goods and services. Consideration is given to improving the product or service, raw materials and supplies, the sequence of operations, tools, the work-place and equipment, and hand and body motions. It is a systematic approach of defining and analysing alternatives, and documenting work methods. Some of the techniques used for work measurement and job simplification are:
  - Process charts and flow diagrams.
  - Operation charts.
  - Micromotion study.
  - Principles of motion economy.
  - Job simplification.
  - Time standards.
  - Value analysis.
  - Operation research techniques.
  - Human factors.
  - Standard data (MTM).
  - Rating schemes.
  - Stopwatch method.
  - Work sampling.

Operations improvement focuses on improving the technical efficiency and effectiveness of specific units. Techniques such as work measurement and procedure design are used to identify potential areas for cost reduction. Work measurement is a means of determining an equitable relationship between the quantity of the work performed and the number of labour hours required for completing that quantity of work. The establishment of measurement is for the purpose of planning, scheduling, and controlling work. Organisations should tailor their staff functions to have work measurement techniques that will help to achieve the following objectives:

- Acquaint staff personnel in charge with more formal methods of productivity management and labour performance.
- The standard developed by work measurement should include standard allowances for rest, delays that occur as part of the job, time for personal needs, and, where the work is heavy, an allowance for personal fatigue.
- Each employee should be involved. Each one should be shown the part to play if formal methods are to be used successfully.
- All participants should be given the confidence that the formal methods do work and should be used.

If carefully implemented, a work measurement programme will help an organisation to achieve the following:

- A tool for decision-making.
- Data provided for scheduling day-to-day operations.
- A basis for labour cost control.

Incentive systems

The approach attempts to focus on methods and techniques for motivating individuals and work groups at different organisational levels. Items such as management style, interpersonal relations, employee relations, dismissal procedures, unemployment insurance, job safety, grievance procedures and dismissal procedures are reviewed periodically and enhancements are made to the programme in order to improve employee or work group productivity. The three most commonly used motivation approaches are the traditional economic incentive approach, the human relations approach and the self-drive approach. Each of these focuses on rewards, satisfying needs, motivating people, assessing impact of chosen strategy and tailoring managerial incentives to achieve results.

Organisation restructuring

This approach focuses on finding better patterns for arranging and structuring organisational activities to reduce waste, cut losses of production and services, and improve overall effectiveness. Emphasis is usually placed on providing the appropriate span of control for operational units, contracting of activities and services, vendor selection programmes, intervention and plan work consolidation and workload elimination.

Technological innovation

This approach concentrates on improving productivity and quality through breakthrough in technological innovation. The usefulness of existing and emerging technologies are continually analysed and improved. The improvement process focuses on both the hardware and software aspects of technology and their capabilities to make work easier and more productive.

Goal clarification

This approach focuses on identifying specific goals and objectives that will improve productivity, implementing these objectives, tracking perform- ance and overtime, and providing on-going assessment of the strengths and weaknesses of an organisation. Questionnaires and opinion surveys are often used as assessment tools. Techniques such as management by objectives and goal structuring are used during the planning process.

Helping the working employee

This approach focuses on identifying specific people- or product-oriented problems that affect employee performance. Specific techniques such as financial incentives, fringe benefits, job enlargement, job enrichment, job training, job rotation, punishment, quality circles, improvement of work- ing conditions, learning curve, management by objectives, employee pro- motions and participative management are used to address issues affecting performance of employees.

Improving the task at the operational unit level

This approach focuses on thorough analysis of each task and elements at the operational unit level. The purpose of the task analysis is to eliminate bar- riers and bottlenecks that affect productivity and quality. Techniques such as methods analysis, job redesign, work measurement, job evaluation, job safety improvement, human factors engineering, data processing improve- ment, workload balancing, task prioritisation and task analysis and improvement are used.

Improving the material usage at operational unit level

This approach attempts to maximise the effective and efficient utilisation of the material. Resource techniques such as parts evaluation, material recycling, inventory control, material requirements planning are used.

Improving the product and service offerings

This approach focuses on providing the most competitive product or service that could be offered to the consumers at the lowest possible cost. Techniques such as value engineering, product diversification, service complexity evaluation, product coding techniques and service quality improvement tools are used.

Improving technology at the operational unit level

This approach focuses on selecting, justifying and implementing appropriate technologies that improve productivity and quality at the task level. Technologies such as robotics, computer graphics, computer-aided manufacturing, laser systems, insertion equipments, energy conservation technology and maintenance technologies are used to improve productivity and quality.

Summary

Productivity and quality improvement at the source requires commitment and training by management, employees, and unions on:

- Adequate process mechanisms to respond effectively to customer requirements.
- Adequate methods and techniques to provide service to the customer.
- Empathy for delivering the right product and service to the customer.
- Knowledge and procedure to deliver products and services on time at minimum cost.
- Customer-needs assessment and assurance to satisfy those needs.
- Adequate delivery processes that guarantee service reliability and appropriate response to both internal and external customers.

The productivity and quality management task boundaries summarised in Fig 1.9 require continuous attention and process improvement. Through such ongoing process improvement, operational units are able to achieve excellence in products and services offered. The productivity and quality principles and guidelines presented in this section are recommended to be used as part of the mechanisms to build productivity and quality improvement philosophy into the organisational culture and into the daily habits of performing work.

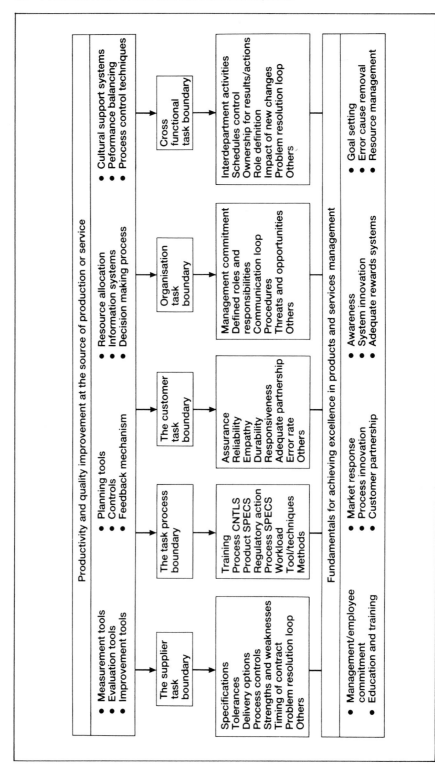

Fig. 1.9 Productivity and quality management task boundaries.

Suggested reading

ASQC, (1971). *Quality Costs – What and How.* American Society for Quality Control, 2nd edn. Milwaukee, WI.

Blank, Lee (1978). Using quality cost analysis for management improvement. *Industrial Engineering,* February.

Deming, W. Edwards (1982). *Quality, Productivity and Competitive Position.* MIT Press, Boston.

Edosomwan, Johnson A. Just-in-time total productivity and quality management. Working Paper, *IBM Technical Publications.*

Edosomwan, Johnson A. The effect of technology on the relationship between productivity and quality. Working Paper, *International Journal of Technology Management.*

Edosomwan, Johnson A. (1986). Statistical process control in group techology production environment. *SYNERGY,* SME Publications.

Edosomwan, Johnson A. (1986). A conceptual framework for productivity planning. *Industrial Engineering,* January.

Edosomwan, Johnson A. (1986). Productivity management in computer-aided manufacturing environment. *Proceedings for the First International Conference on Engineering Management, Arlington, Virginia,* September 1986.

Edosomwan, Johnson A. (1986). Statistical process control in electronics printed circuit board asembly. *Proceedings for the Annual Fall Industrial Engineering Conference, Boston, Mass.,* December 1986.

Edosomwan, Johnson A. (1986). Productivity and quality management – a challenge in the year 2000. *Proceedings for the Annual International Industrial Engineering Conference, Boston, Mass.,* December 1986.

Edosomwan, Johnson A. (1987). *Integrating Productivity and Quality Management.* Marcel Dekker Inc., New York, New York.

Edosomwan, Johnson A. (1987). A program for managing productivity and quality. *Industrial Engineering,* January.

Edosomwan, Johnson A. (1987). The challenge for industrial managers: productivity and quality in the work place. *Industrial Management,* September/October.

Edosomwan, Johnson A. Understanding the connection between productivity and quality in a competitive business environment. Keynote Address presented in the proceedings for the IFS Conference on SPC, Birmingham, England, November 1987.

Edosomwan, Johnson A. Improving productivity and quality at the source. Proceedings for the Annual International Industrial Engineering Conference. 18–25 May, 1988, Orlando, Florida.

Juran, J.M. and Gryna, F.M., Jr (1980). *Quality Planning and Analysis.* McGraw-Hill Book Company, New York.

Kendrick, John W. (1984). *Improving Company Productivity: A Handbook with Case Studies.* The Johns Hopkins University Press, Baltimore, MD.

Zubairi, M. Mazhar (1985). Statistical process control management issues. *Proceedings for the Annual International Industrial Engineering Conference.*

2 JUST-IN-TIME QUALITY ASSESSMENT AND IMPROVEMENT TOOLS

Statistical process control

Statistical process control (SPC) provides a disciplined approach whereby statistical inference techniques are used to monitor and control process variation. The control concept utilises statistical measurement of process variation to control and minimise defects. The implementation of SPC is achieved by providing:

- Control system for defect detection.
- Control system for error cause removal.
- Control system for error analysis.
- Control system for defect analysis.

Through the implementation of SPC the following benefits can be derived:

- A process control system is in place to provide feedback about process characteristics, variables and overall performance.
- A basis is provided for detecting chance and assignable causes that affect process performance.

- A basis is provided for understanding the interaction among process variables and therefore able to improve their performance.
- A basis is provided for minimising the cost of quality.

The following steps are recommended for implementing statistical process control:

- **Step one:** Understand the current process thoroughly including the key inputs and outputs utilised for production or service.
- **Step two:** Classify production or service process into operational units or work cells.
- **Step three:** Identify specific quality and productivity problems within each cell. This can be done by performing a thorough input and output analysis for each operational unit.
- **Step four:** Formulate the specific quality and problem.
- **Step five:** Identify possible problem causes or potential improvement actions. Use cause and effect diagrams to identify root cause of problem and possible effects on the process performance.
- **Step six:** Develop measurement method for process variables.
- **Step seven:** Design data collection system and database for process information.
- **Step eight:** Train personnel on process measurement methods and data collection instruments.
- **Step nine:** Collect and synthesise data from existing and new process.
- **Step ten:** Organise data using histograms, Pareto charts, graphs, tables and charts.
- **Step eleven:** Compute process control limits using attribute and variable control chart formulas.
- **Step twelve:** Analyse results and interpret control charts for process capability and possible assignable causes.
- **Step thirteen:** Improve the process performance by taking corrective action to fix root cause of problem identified.
- **Step fourteen:** Monitor the process continuously for continuous improvement.

Histogram

The frequency histogram can be described as a bar graph displaying the frequency distribution of specific processes, items, and devices. The tool provides a valuable means for tracking variation. For instance, the histogram might be used to categorise product defect levels or distribution. (See Fig. 2.1 for an example). A frequency histogram provides the basis for understanding the variation of both production and service scenarios with the visualisation to identify opportunity easily with each area (histograph

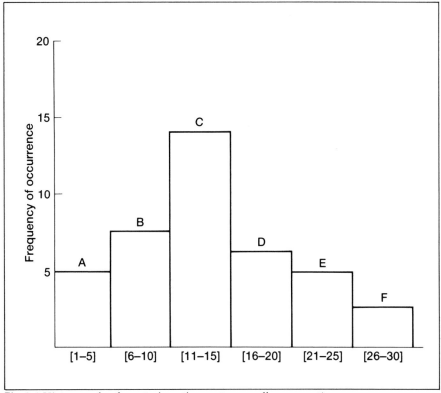

Fig. 2.1 Histogram for the auto-insertion customer call response time.

bars) while keeping track of variation. It must be pointed out that frequency histograms do not tell the total sources of variation and do not present a specific pattern over time.

How to construct a frequency histogram

A frequency histogram can be constructed by using the following illustrative steps and example provided:

- **Step one: Obtain and record a clear definition for the subject.** In this step, the item(s), device, characteristics or process which require a frequency histogram to be constructed is defined. For example, in 1979 a medium-sized company decided to understand and classify the frequency of the response time to customer calls when a high technology insertion machine breaks down. The subject in this example is the customer calls response time for the insertion machine.
- **Step two: Design, test, and establish data collection procedure.** This step is concerned with the provision of an adequate data collection procedure for recording information. In order for the data collected to be meaningful, about 20 to 100 observations are recommended. The

data collected should represent homogeneous conditions of the process or subject considered. For the auto-insertion customer calls response time example, the 40 observations obtained are presented in Table 2.1.

- **Step three: Calculate the Range of Measurement.** First circle the largest and smallest number in each group/set and then calculate the range using the formula presented here:

Range value = (highest value − lowest value)

From the example, the range is (30 − 129).

- **Step four: Determine histogram width.** The histogram width is obtained by adding 1 to the range; this is the number required to include all other numerical values. From the example width is (29 + 1 = 30).

- **Step five: Decide the number of bars in the histogram.** The number of bars is obtained by an approximation technique after careful examination of the total number of observations. The idea is to have the observations classified by groups or bars that represent the entire observations. Table 2.2 presents a guide for determining the number of bars based on total number of observations.

- **Step six: Derive class interval.** The class interval is computed by using the following formula:

$$\text{Histogram class interval} = \frac{\text{histogram width}}{\text{number of bars}}$$

From the example, histogram class interval = 30/6 = 5.

Table 2.1 *Auto-insertion machine: customer calls response time in minutes: 40 observations used in the construction of histograms*

1	4	2	7	8
9	23	18	13	25
16	24	12	13	12
13 ·	17	21	10	19
6	5	30	11	9
15	11	14	27	7
13	17	12	22	16
14	4	6	20	14

Table 2.2 *Guide for deriving histogram bars*

Number of observations	Number of bars
Under 30	3–5
30–50	5–7
50–100	6–10
100–250	7–13
250–1000 (over)	10–25

Table 2.3 Frequencies for the auto-insertion customer call response time

Bar	Interval	Tallies	Total
1	1–5	|||||	5
2	6–10	||||| |||	8
3	11–15	||||| ||||| |||	13
4	16–20	||||| ||	7
5	21–25	|||||	5
6	26–30	||	2
Total		40	40

- **Step seven: Derive and establish class boundaries.** The class boundaries are obtained by using the following procedure:
  - Assume lowest number in the total observations is boundary one.
  - The value of boundary one plus the class width becomes boundary two value.
  - The successive boundary determination process is continued until the total number of boundaries becomes equal to the total number of bars.
- **Step eight: Tabulate the histogram frequencies.** In this step, the various observations are failed into appropriate bars. Table 2.3 shows how the recording process is performed. If the tabulation process is done correctly, the total failed should be equal to the total number of observations.

- **Step nine: Construct the histogram.** The histogram is constructed by devising two axis chart as shown in Fig. 2.1. The Y-axis of the chart should represent the frequency of occurrence while the X-axis should represent the various intervals. An appropriate scale should be used to accommodate the total number of occurrences. By connecting the total points plotted on the graph, one can see pictorially the histogram bars.
- **Step ten: Interpret histogram spread.** In this step the bar graphs are analysed to provide an understanding of the specific magnitude of each area. From the example presented, most of the customer response times can be seen to occur between 8 and 13 minutes. This information enables us to see the distribution of the customer call response time as well as specific variations.

Pareto analysis

A Pareto diagram can be described as a graphical representation of identified causes, shown in descending order of magnitude or frequency. The magnitude of concern is usually plotted against the category of concern. (See Fig. 2.2 for an example.)

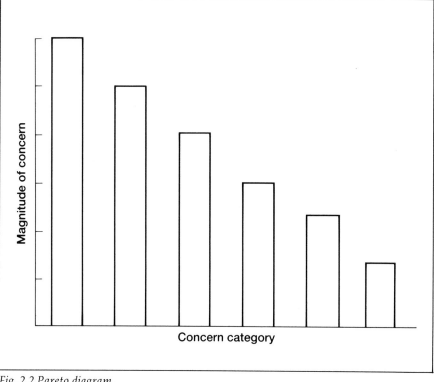

Fig. 2.2 Pareto diagram.

The Pareto diagram enables the process improvement analyst to identify the vital few problems, projects or issues to concentrate on. By doing so, resources are allocated to resolve the most important problems. It also provides the basis for identifying the magnitude of the problem that can be eliminated by correcting the most vital few important issues. It is a valuable tool for deciding on which problem to resolve first and what resources should be expanded and approved by management. This tool relies heavily on the ranking process and histogram distribution.

How to construct a Pareto diagram

The following steps are recommended for constructing a Pareto diagram:

- **Step one: Specify why a Pareto diagram is required.** A clear definition of the items to be ranked, the criteria to be used, and the factor should be specified. Usually, the motivation for Pareto analysis comes from complex and too many problems occurring within an operation unit or a specific process. The Pareto diagram is then used to categorise the various problems in their order of magnitude. For example, in 1987 a printed circuit board (PCB) manufacturer wanted to understand the repair and analysis cost associated with the various specific types of

PCBs. Pareto analysis technique was applied to understand the magnitude of this problem.

- **Step two: Perform data collection and record by item.** In this step, the number of occurrences of each problem and the associated magnitude in weight, cost or time are collected and recorded. For the PCB example, the repair and analysis cost for each type of PCB is presented in Table 2.4.

- **Step three: Calculate percentages for each item and rank order.** The percentages for each item and the total cumulative percentages for all items are calculated as follows:

$$\text{Item \%} = \frac{\text{each item (weight or value)}}{\text{total items (weight or value)}}$$

Cumulative % = (each item % + cumulative %)

For the PCB example, the product and cumulative percentages are presented in Table 2.5.

- **Step four: Construct graph axes and plot bars and cumulative % line.** Based on the values of items obtained in step three the Pareto diagram is constructed. For the PCB example, the Pareto diagram is presented in Fig. 2.3.

Table 2.4 Repair and analysis cost for printed circuit boards

PCB types	Defect occurrence (total number)	Cost per occurrence	Total cost per PCB type ($)
PCB 1	15	20	300
PCB 2	18	40	720
PCB 3	20	10	200
PCB 4	14	5	70
PCB 5	10	10	100
PCB 6	5	25	125
Total	82		1515

Table 2.5 Product and cumulative costs for printed circuit boards

PCB	Repair and analysis cost ($)	Product (%)	Cumulative (%)
PCB 2	720	47.5	47.5
PCB 1	300	19.8	67.3
PCB 3	200	13.2	80.5
PCB 6	125	8.3	88.8
PCB 5	100	6.6	95.4
PCB 4	70	4.6	100.0
Total	1515	100.0	

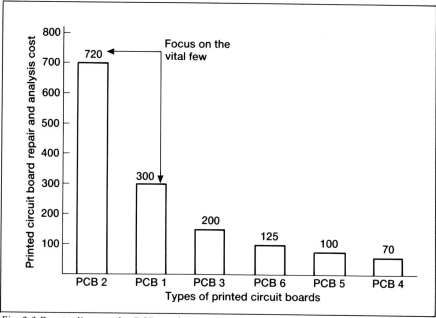

Fig. 2.3 Pareto diagram for PCB products.

Cause-and-effect diagram

The cause-and-effect diagram shown in Fig. 2.4 relates possible causes to specific effect. All the possible causes that add to the variation level of the resultant effect are identified using a brainstorming approach.

The following steps can be used in constructing the cause-and-effect diagram.

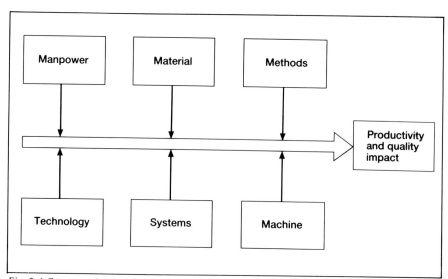

Fig. 2.4 Cause-and-effect diagram.

- **Step one:** Define the purpose and problem for using the cause-and-effect diagram.
- **Step two:** Initiate group meeting involving all parties likely or known to be affected by the problem.
- **Step three:** Have group brainstorm on all possible cause(s) of the specific problem and perform process impact analysis.
- **Step four:** Determine the main cause(s) of the problem by each operational unit.
- **Step five:** Develop solutions strategies for fixing the problem, implement the solution, and follow-up with corrective action.

Matrix analysis technique

The matrix analysis technique is useful in assessing the magnitude of errors by different source points. The error types are classified by task or employee. The Employee-Error Matrix (EEM) shows the magnitude of each error type by employee while the Task-Error Matrix (TEM) shows the magnitude of each error type by task. An example of the TEM is presented in Table 2.6. The five common types of errors that can be documented and analysed with EEM and TEM are:

- **Wilful errors.** These are errors caused intentionally by the employee. For example, an employee may fail to use the prescribed tools, process or technique in performing a task. Wilful errors can be fixed through counselling and training.
- **Inadvertent errors.** These are errors that employees cannot avoid, due to inability to maintain attention. Inadvertent errors can be corrected through training in concentration and by task redesign.
- **Technique errors.** These are errors caused by lack of the right skills to perform the required task. Again this type of error can be eliminated by providing proper training.

Table 2.6 Task error matrix for a typical parts assembly unit

Error type	Task					
	Assembly stage one	*Assembly stage two*	*Cover assembly*	*Product test*	*Pack and ship*	*Total*
Missing components	4	5	15	0	0	24
Defective screws	1	1	0	0	0	2
Too much unit vibration	3	3	4	1	0	11
Loosen screws	8	2	10	10	14	44
Wrong packaging label	1	11	3	1	16	32
Electric shock on system	0	0	1	23	1	25
Total	17	22	33	35	31	

- **Policies errors.** These errors are caused by management or by the operating procedures and policies set by management. Only management can correct these types of errors. Usually policies and procedures have to be rewritten or re-evaluated and revised for clarity.
- **Environmental errors.** These are errors caused by the environmental influence, for example, tight regulation by the government on specific product specifications. These errors are usually corrected through adjustment of processes to the environmental regulations.

Capability ratio

The capability ratio is used to establish the standard for new machinery, prioritise the assignment of inspection and repair personnel, and determine gauging frequencies.

$$\text{Capability ratio} = \frac{\text{capability}}{\text{part print tolerance}}$$

The mini-capability study estimates the overall machine capability. It is an excellent problem identification tool. The following steps are recommended for performing a mini-capability study.

- **Step one:** Collect a sample of ten consecutive parts.
- **Step two:** Measure the parts to obtain a real reading on the study characteristics. Record the values obtained.
- **Step three:** Determine the range. The range is obtained by the highest value of a sample of ten, minus the lowest value.
- **Step four:** Multiply the range by a factor of two. This estimates the width of the bell curve, plus and minus three standard deviations.
- **Step five:** Use the average of the sample of ten readings to locate the centre of the distribution.

The process control value based on the capability ratio is presented in Table 2.7. The various classes presented can be used to determine which operation is excellent, good, fair or poor.

Table 2.7 Process control value based on capability ratio

Operation class	A (excellent)	B (good)	C (fair)	D (poor)
Machine capability as a percent of total process tolerance	50% or less	51% to 70%	71% to 90%	91% and over
Gauging frequency operator	Normal	Normal	Frequent	100%
Gauging frequency (floor inspector)	Seldom	Normal	Frequent	Very frequent
Control chart	Optional	Optional	Required	Required
Pre-control system	Optional	Optional	Actual reading used for charts	Gauge are control

Conducting a process capability study

The following steps are recommended for conducting a process capability study:

- **Step one:** Collect a random sample of a minimum of fifty observations from the process.
- **Step two:** Calculate the mean and standard deviation of the sample values.

$$\text{Mean} \;=\; \bar{X} \;=\; \sum_{i=1}^{n} \frac{X_i}{N}$$

$$\text{Standard deviation} \;=\; S \;=\; \sqrt{\frac{\sum_{i=1}^{N} (X_i - \bar{X})^2}{N-1}}$$

where X_i = value of individual sample, N = total number of values in the collection.

- **Step three:** Calculate the process capability by using the following formula.

$$\text{Process capability} \;=\; 6S$$

- **Step four:** If a normal distribution is assumed, calculate the upper and lower capability limit by using the following formulae:

$$\text{Upper capability limit} \;=\; \bar{X} + 3S$$
$$\text{Lower capability limit} \;=\; \bar{X} - 3S$$

The average range method can also be used for estimating process capability.

$$\bar{R} \;=\; \frac{\sum_{i=1}^{N_1} Ri}{N}$$

where $\bar{R}$ = the range of the sample, R_i = the range of the ith sample, N = the number of samples taken.

The standard deviation estimate S^1 can be obtained as follows:

$$S^1 \;=\; \frac{\bar{R}}{d_2}$$

The factor d_2 depends on the sample size, and can be obtained using the values specified in Table 2.8. The process capability can therefore be obtained as follows:

$$\text{Process capability} \quad 6S^1$$

Table 2.8 d_2 values based on sample size n

n	d_2
2	1.128
3	1.693
4	2.059
5	2.326
6	2.534
7	2.704
8	2.847
9	2.970
10	3.078
11	3.173
12	3.258
13	3.336
14	3.407
15	3.472

Control charts

Control charts are statistical devices used for monitoring the output of a process or system through the sample measurement of a specific characteristic and the analysis of its performance over time. Control charts are used to study variations in a process that are attributed to special causes. Variation can be defined as the degree to which process output and yield are not identical. The primary goal in the use of control charts is to reduce fluctuation in a process until it is in a state of statistical process control. Figures 2.5 and 2.6 present typical control charts. There are two types of control charts used to study variation in a process: these are attribute and variable control charts.

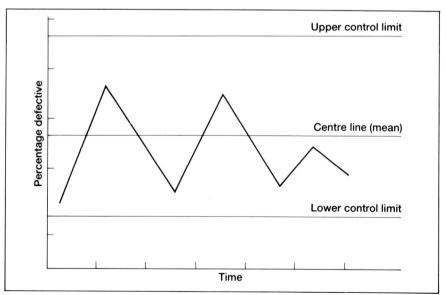

Fig. 2.5 Typical control chart.

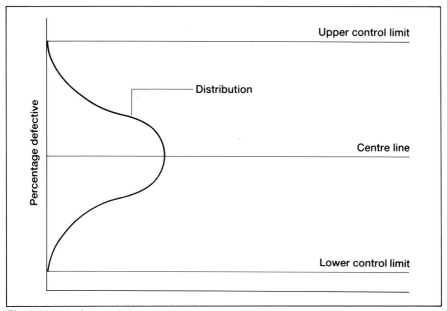

Fig. 2.6 Typical control chart and distribution.

Attribute control charts

Attribute control charts measure whether the product is defective, based on a number of quality characteristics. The attribute of interest can be based on a unit containing one or more defects or one source of failure to meet specified requirement. The four types of attribute control charts commonly used are described below:

The P chart (fraction defective control chart)

The *P* chart is based on attribute data average number of defective units of product. It is used to control the overall defective fraction of a process. The *P* chart provides the proportion of defective product in a sample and is based on a binomial distribution. It is recommended when sample sizes are not equivalent. The data points, process average and control limits are presented below:

$$\text{Datapoints,} P = \frac{\text{number of defective units}}{\text{number of units in sample}}$$

$$\text{Process average, } \bar{P} = \frac{\text{total defect units}}{\text{total units observed}}$$

$$\text{Upper control limit; UCL} = \bar{P} + 3\sqrt{\frac{\bar{P}(1 - \bar{P})}{n}}$$

$$\text{Lower control limit; LCL} = \bar{P} - 3\sqrt{\frac{\bar{P}(1 - \bar{P})}{n}}$$

The *np* chart

The *np* chart is used to measure the number of defectives in a sample of constant size. The data points, process average and control limits are presented below:

Data points, np = number of defective units in sample

Process average = $np = \dfrac{\text{total defective units}}{\text{number of samples}}$

Upper control limit, UCL = $\bar{n}\bar{p} + 3\sqrt{\bar{n}\bar{p}(1 - \bar{p})}$

Lower control limit, LCL = $\bar{n}\bar{p} - 3\sqrt{\bar{n}\bar{p}(1 - \bar{p})}$

C chart

The C chart is used to measure the number of defects in a sample when the opportunity in each area is equivalent for each sample. More than one defect may be recorded on a piece in the sample; the C value can be defined as the number of defects in a constant sample size. The data points, process average and control limits are presented below:

Data points, C = number of defects in sample

Process average, $\bar{C} = \dfrac{\text{total defects}}{\text{number of samples}}$

Upper control limit, UCL = $\bar{C} + 3\sqrt{\bar{C}}$

Upper control limit, UCL = $\bar{C} - 3\sqrt{\bar{C}}$

U chart

The *U* chart measures the average number of defects in a sample. It is applied when the number of units observed differs from sample to sample. The data points, process average and control limits are presented below:

Data points, U = the ratio of non-conformatives to the sample size.

$U = \dfrac{c}{n}$

$U = \dfrac{\text{number of defects}}{\text{sample size}}$

Process average; $\bar{U} = \dfrac{\text{total number of defects}}{\text{total process accepted}}$

Upper control limit, $\text{UCL} = \bar{U} + 3\sqrt{\dfrac{\bar{U}}{n}}$

Lower control limit, $\text{LCL} = \bar{U} + 3\sqrt{\dfrac{\bar{U}}{n}}$

Variable control charts

The variable control charts measure the degree in variation of a single quality characteristic, such as tolerance, weight, hardness or temperature. These charts cannot be used with go or no-go data. They are helpful when detailed information on the process average and variations is needed for control of individual dimensions. The variable control chart uses an average of a small sample called a rational subgroup. The two most widely used variable control charts are the X chart and the R chart.

The various definitions associated with X and R charts, data points, process averages, control limits, control chart factors and distributions are presented in Tables 2.9, 2.10 and 2.11.

Table 2.9 Definitions and formulae for variable control charts

Let:
X_i = Individual observation
$\bar{X}$ = the mean of a subgroup
R_i = the range of a subgroup
$\bar{\bar{X}}$ = the grand means
$\bar{R}$ = the average subgroup range
N = the number of observations in a subgroup
n = the number of subgroups

Means: sum of observations divided by the number of observations
Range: difference between the largest and smallest number in the total observations
Subgroup: homogeneous small sample unit
Observations: value of a characteristic for individual unit

Chart	Data points	Average line	Upper control limit (UCL)	Lower control limit (LCL)
X	X	$\bar{X} = \dfrac{\sum X_i}{N}$	$\bar{X} + \dfrac{\sum 3\bar{R}}{d_2}$	$\bar{X} = \dfrac{3\bar{R}}{d_2}$
$\bar{X}$	$\dfrac{\sum X_i}{N}$	$\bar{\bar{X}} = \dfrac{\sum \bar{X}_i}{n}$	$\bar{\bar{X}} + A_2\bar{R}$	$\bar{\bar{X}} - A_2\bar{R}$
R	X maximum minus X minimum	$\bar{R} = \dfrac{\sum \bar{R}_i}{n}$	$D_4\bar{R}$	$D_3\bar{R}$

Sample size for attributes and variable control charts

For $\bar{X}$ and range (R) charts the sample size recommended is usually 4 or 5; for per cent defective chart (p) samples of 25, 50 or 100 are recommended from inspection results. For the C chart a sample size of one is recommended.

Table 2.10 Factors for variable control charts (X and R charts)

Sample size (n)	Average (A₂)	Range		Standard deviation (d₂)
		D₃	D₄	
2	1.880	–	3.268	1.128
3	1.023	–	2.574	1.693
4	0.729	–	2.282	2.059
5	0.577	–	2.115	2.326
6	0.483	–	2.004	2.534
7	0.419	0.076	1.924	2.704
8	0.373	0.136	1.864	2.847
9	0.337	0.184	1.816	2.970
10	0.308	0.223	1.777	3.078
11	0.285	0.256	1.744	3.173
12	0.266	0.284	1.717	3.258
13	0.249	0.308	1.692	3.336
14	0.235	0.329	1.671	3.407
15	0.223	0.348	1.652	3.472

Table 2.11 Attribute and variable control charts

Chart	Name	Type of data	Distribution
P	Fraction defective	Attribute	Binomial
np	Number defective	Attribute	Binomial
C	Number of defects	Attribute	Poisson
U	Defects per unit	Attribute	Poisson
X	Individual measurement	Variable	Normal
X̄	Averages	Variable	Normal
R	Ranges	Variable	Normal

Control chart construction

The following steps are recommended for constructing control charts:

- **Step one:** Understand the process from which variation in process output is to be monitored.
- **Step two:** Select the variables to be controlled and charted.
- **Step three:** Determine the size and methods of obtaining subgroups from the process output.
- **Step four:** Choose the type of control chart to be used (P, np, R, C, $\bar{X}$, X, U, etc).
- **Step five:** Collect data and plot until the period is considered representative of the normal operation of the process (30 or more points are desirable).
- **Step six:** Connect the data points for readability.
- **Step seven:** Calculate the centre line of the chart, i.e., the average of the sample.

- **Step eight:** Calculate the upper and lower control limits and set the trial control limits.
- **Step nine:** Revise the control limits based on the age of the data (usually 25 points or more) and the state of the process.

Interpretation of control charts

Control charts are useful tools for detecting assignable causes responsible for process variation. They are only useful if appropriately interpreted and used. The key indicators for reviewing control charts are:

- Process points, process average, upper and lower control limits.
- Variation in process points, trend or patterns.
- Root causes (assignable) for problems.
- Run: successive points on one side or either side of the process average.
- Cycles: a unique pattern of causes.
- Key actions implemented to address process problems.
- Projected improvement based on implemented actions with benefit date.

In evaluating the process runs, the control chart is directed into zones. Each zone is one standard deviation wide. Between the upper and lower control limit is a total of six standard deviations. The centre line divides the control into two zones of three standard deviations each. The various chart zones presented in Fig. 2.7 for applying tests for instability process are determined by the following:

- A single point falls out 3 standard deviations beyond zone *A*.
- Two of three successive points fall in zone *A* or beyond the odd point.

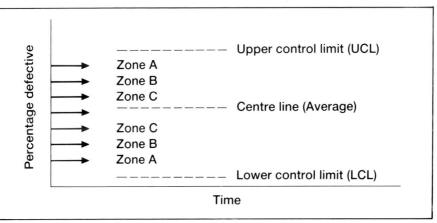

Fig. 2.7 Control chart zones for applying tests for instability.

- Four of five successive points in zone B or beyond.
- Eight successive points fall in zone C or beyond.
- One or more points are outside the upper and lower control limits on the charts.
- A run of 7 or more points above or below the process average central line.
- Cycle or non-random patterns of the data points on the charts.
- Eight successive points on the same side.
- Any 11 or 12 successive points on the same side.
- Any 13 or 15 successive points on the same side.

Definition of assignable cause(s)

Assignable causes responsible for variation in a process average perform-ance may be monitored by points attributed to special causes such as:

- Differences among machines.
- Differences among operators.
- Operators skill level.
- Differences in product.
- Influence of external factors.
- Interrelationship among process variables.
- Introduction of new process.
- Introduction of new product.
- Instability in performance rates.
- Imbalance in process parameters.

Environmental constraint cause(s)

These are factors which influence the process performance but cannot be altered directly by changes within the process. Example are regulations and specifications.

Continuation cause(s)

Continuation causes are responsible for variations in the process which cause on-going problems in particular aspects of the process. These types of causes are best solved by understanding the (inter)relationship among pro-cess parameters.

Maintainable cause(s)

Maintainable causes are responsible for variations in the process that cause monitored points to be maintained at a given level.

Sporadic cause(s)

Sporadic causes are responsible for large variations in the process perfor-mance monitored by points that exhibit random occurrences.

The process and equipment characterisation methods help us under-stand the effect of fixture, adjustment of tools and equipment impact on the final output. Process characterisation provides a unique approach for detecting possible assignable causes before they develop. It usually reveals frequency of occurrence for machine and tool-related defects, and frequency of defect occurrence due to adjustments.

Design of experiments

When the assignable causes responsible for process variation become difficult to isolate, experiments are usually designed. The three basic principles of experimental design are as follows:

- Replication involves repetition of a basic experiment. The experimental error can be estimated, and a sample mean can be a useful tool to obtain a precise estimate of parameters.
- Randomisation involves the allocation of the experimental material and the order in which an individual runs the experiment. These are randomly determined.
- Blocking involves making comparisons among the conditions of interest in the experiment within each block. It is used to increase the precision of an experiment.

The following steps are recommended for designing experiments:

- **Step one:** The process problem and area of impact are identified. Historical evidence of the existence of a problem or an estimate of trends to support the definition of a problem must be provided. Other interrelated variables that need further clarification must also be specified.
- **Step two:** The specific problem statements are translated to null and alternative hypotheses to enable the data obtained to be analysed statistically.
- **Step three:** The planning and implementation of the experiment will be successful if all personnel involved in the problem area of impact have involvement in specifying variables, factors, and parameters. This provides a clear idea of what is studied, how all relevant information is obtained, and the usefulness of the result of the experiment. The resources needed to perform and implement the results of the experiment are also easily obtained through co-operation from everyone involved.
- **Step four:** In this step a distinction is made between quantitative and qualitative factors, dependent and independent variables, and the range over which all factors and variables are selected. Other parameters, such as the number of levels of runs and factor interaction, are selected.
- **Step five:** All dependent variables are clearly specified. Dependent variables and other variables must be selected based on facts, not opinions. The measurement methods for each variable should be specified.

- **Step six:** It is important to note that complicated experiments are expensive in terms of both increased possibility of error and increased cost. It is recommended that experimental design be kept as simple as possible. The choice of experimental design must be based on the following factors: cost, risk, accuracy level, and the true response range of all resources needed for the detection of causes assignable to the problem being investigated.
- **Step seven:** In this step, particular attention must be paid to randomisation, measurement accuracy, and maintaining the experimental environment as uniform as possible. Appropriate measurement instruments must be designed for data collection and there must be random checks on the validity of the data source and frequency.
- **Step eight:** Data should be collected periodically based on the specified time-table for the experiment. The data should be syn-thesised and all unnecessary information weeded out.
- **Step nine:** In this step, statistical techniques, such as the analysis of variance (ANOVA), and other simple tools, such as mean and variances, are used to analyse the data collected from the experiment. The techniques must be able to specify the range of validity or significance of the results obtained from the experiment. The statistical techniques used must be able to show a confidence interval for results. Computer programs and graphic analysis techniques should be employed when applicable to eliminate tedious manual computations.
- **Step ten:** The conclusions and recommendations from the experiment must be drawn from the results obtained. The practical significance and implications of the results and findings must be clearly stated. Recommended actions to resolve the problem investigated must be specified. The exposures and limitations of findings and recommendations must be pointed out to avoid further problems when solutions are implemented.

Inspection and sampling

Productivity and quality improvement at the source requires that the job be done right the first time. 100%, 200% and triple inspection should be discouraged because they have no added value to the product. In most cases inspection creates more defect. To avoid inspection cost the following techniques are recommended:

- Provide the right training.
- Provide the right tools and equipment.
- Let everyone take ownership for results.
- Do not put pressure on people to produce more than their acceptable limits.

- Give clear definitions of roles, responsibilities, and levels of achievement.
- Let everyone ensure that no output goes to internal and external customers unless it is perfect. Everyone must inspect his own work. The line must stop if the process is out of control.
- Do not use an out of control process for production or service.
- Make sure that the total problem can be assigned to known causes responsible for process variations.

Sampling technique is a means of selecting random units from lots or batches. Sampling by variables requires data on specific measurements, while sampling by attributes requires go or no-go decisions. The following types of sampling plan are most widely used:

Attribute sampling plan

Attribute sampling plan can be defined by three numbers: N = the number of units in the lot (of size); n = the number of units in the sample; c = the acceptance number.

If we let X = the number of defectives in the sample and P^1 = fraction defective in the lot, the fraction defective in the sample (P) will be:

$$P = \frac{X}{n}$$

Single sampling plan

This procedure requires a sample of size n to be taken at random from a lot.

Let X = the number of defectives in the sample and C = critical number of defectives.

Decision rule.

If $X \leqslant C$ accept lot
If $X > C$ reject lot

Double and multiple sampling plans

These sampling procedures are designed to obtain a decision after the first sample is taken. The second sample is used to reject or accept the lot.

Let N = number of units in the lot (lot size), n_1 = size of sample 1, n_2 = size of sample 2, c_1 = acceptance number for the first sample, that is the maximum number of defectives used to make acceptance decision after the first sample, C_2 = acceptance number for two samples combined, X_1 = number of defectives in sample 1, X_2 = number of defectives in sample 2.

Decision rules.
Rule 1: When a sample of size ni is taken from the lot and X_1 is obtained,

> If $X_1 \leqslant C_1$ accept lot
> If $X_1 > C_2$ reject lot
> If $C_1 < X_1 \leqslant C_2$ must take sample 2

Rule 2: When sample 2 is taken, the number of defectives in the second sample is added to the number of defectives in the first,

> If $X_1 + X_2 \leqslant C_2$ accept lot
> If $X_1 + X_2 > C_2$ reject lot

Cluster sampling

This procedure involves the use of a random number table to select groups of items and then samples within each cluster. It is recommended for stable processes.

Sampling plans are usually described by an operating characteristics curve that presents the probability of accepting a lot under a specific type of plan for a specific quality characteristic or variable. Figure 2.8 presents a typical operating characteristics curve.

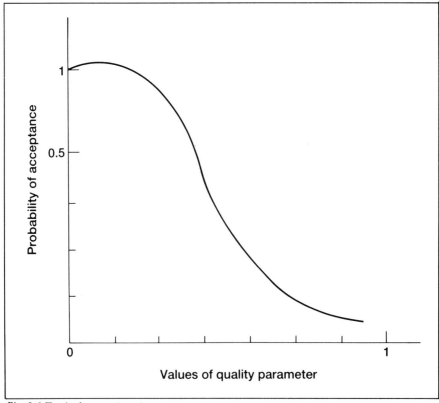

Fig. 2.8 Typical operating characteristics curve.

Table 2.12 Errors and risks in sampling

	Good	Bad
Accept	Correct decision	Type II error: consumer's risk = β
Reject	Type I error: producer's risk (α)	Correct decision

Errors and risks in sampling

There are two types of errors in sampling:

- Type I error: A decision is made to reject a good lot, that is, one that should be accepted.
- Type II error: A decision is made to accept a bad lot, one that should be rejected.

The probability of making a type I error is called producer's risk, while the probability of making a type II error is called consumer's risk. The two types of errors and associated risks are presented in Table 2.12.

Average outgoing quality (AOQ)

The average outgoing quality (AOQ) measures the effectiveness of an acceptance sampling plan. AOQ can be obtained as follows:

Let: P_A = probability of acceptance and P_I = fraction defective of

$$AOQ = P_I \cdot P_A$$

Scatter diagram

A scatter diagram can be described as a graph displaying the correlation of two characteristics.

Examples of scatter diagrams are presented in Fig. 2.9. The scatter diagram can be used to determine if a cause-and-effect relationship might exist. The following steps are recommended for constructing scatter diagrams:

- **Step one:** Define the specific process problem which requires correlation analysis.
- **Step two:** Collect data on specific measurements and process element values such as pressure and temperature.
- **Step three:** Tabulate and plot the points on graph paper.

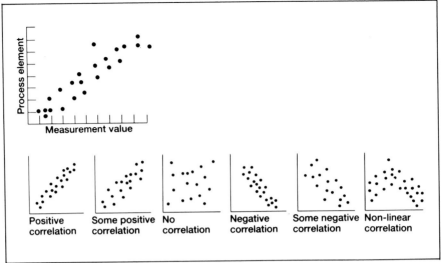

Fig 2.9 Examples of scatter diagrams.

- **Step four:** Interpret the graphs for levels of correlation. The interpretation pattern may follow positive, negative, no correlation or non-linear correlation.
- **Step five:** Use the correlation analysis to diagnose the specific problem when seeking to know whether a cause-and-effect relationship might exist.

Hypothesis testing

Hypothesis testing procedures involve the collection of sample data which are used to calculate test statistics. The data collected are used to validate certain assertions about a particular process. The following definitions and concepts are important when discussing hypothesis testing:

- **Null hypothesis:** The null hypothesis (H0) assumes that there is no difference between specified population parameters.
- **Alternative hypothesis:** The alternative hypothesis (H1) assumes that there is a difference between specified population parameters.
- **Critical region:** The critical region for H0 is defined as the range of values of the test statistic that corresponds to a rejection of the hypothesis at some fixed probability of committing a type I error.
- **Type I error:** This sampling error occurs when a true hypothesis is rejected. The probability of a type I error is usually denoted by α.
- **Type II error:** This sampling error occurs when a false hypothesis is accepted. The probability of a type II error is usually denoted by β.

- **Test statistics:** The test statistics used for hypothesis testing are determined by the specific probability distribution sampled and by the parameters selected (mean, variance, standard deviation etc.) for testing.
- **Hypothesis-testing situation:** The following are the most common situations considered in hypothesis testing:

  - Comparison of sample means when the variance of the population is known.
  - Comparison of sample means of normal distributions when the variance of the population is unknown.
  - Comparison of variance of normal distributions.
  - Comparison of parameters of binomial distribution.
  - Comparison of parameters of Poisson distribution.

The following procedure and steps are recommended for testing a hypothesis:

- **Step one:** Specify the appropriate probability model for the outcomes of the random experiment under investigation. The choice of a model should be based on significant experience in observing the performance of the particular process or based on the best judgement.
- **Step two:** State the null and alternative hypothesis in terms of the population parameters.
- **Step three:** Select appropriate test statistics and specify the sample size.
- **Step four:** Select a value of type I error and define the region of rejection and acceptance. Choose the specific level for α.
- **Step five:** Perform data collection for all variables and parameters.
- **Step six:** Determine the distribution of test statistics.
- **Step seven:** Compute the test statistics using the appropriate formulae (see Appendix B) for hypothesis formulae.
- **Step eight:** Compare the value of the acceptance region and decide whether to accept or reject the hypothesis.
- **Step nine:** Interpret the results from the analysis. Accept or reject H0 by comparing the value of the test statistics with the value of the critical region.
- **Step ten:** Draw the conclusion based on the interpretation of results.

The most commonly used statistical formulae for hypothesis testing are presented in Appendix B.

Quality error removal (QER) technique

The quality error removal (QER) technique is a unique type of quality circle approach to problem solving and resolution at the source of production and service. Unlike the typical quality circle that is run free-wheel, the QER technique provides organised guide lines, framework and principles to a group of workers (managers and non-managers) who voluntarily decide to work together to select and solve production or service problems affecting the performance of an organisation's work unit or task. The QER technique requires that organisational goals be broken down into specific small tasks at the operational unit level, and continuous effort is then applied to improve productivity and quality within each work unit. Adherence to the following principles is recommended when using the QER technique:

Principle one: teach workers basic job skills and cross-train for multiple skills

Both employees and management will be convinced that productivity and quality improvement is possible in an organisation and within each task unit, once everyone involved understands how the job should be performed to deliver a good product. Everyone also understands the nature of the product or services being delivered. Two types of training are encouraged: formal training through a company educational programme or an outside institution, and training by peers.

Principle two: encourage decision-making and problem-solving at the source of production or services

At the operational level, the QER terms select their own problems on which to focus and decide how to attack the bottle-neck issues that are preventing productivity and quality improvement. The team identifies problems over which there is control. All members of the team freely contribute ideas and reach a consensus on the best possible solution. The brainstorming technique is highly encouraged. The following steps are followed to understand the cause and effect of a key problem.

- Define the problem precisely.
- Draw a flow diagram, and label all categories.
- Brainstorm to identify the root cause of the problem.
- Use a Pareto diagram to select a problem on which to focus.
- Obtain consensus on a solution.
- Implement the solution and follow-up on issues.

Principle three: encourage productivity and quality improvement at the source of production or service

Each product or service inspection is done at the source. Inspection is on the line at the task level. Members of the QER team perform inspection of their own work. Quality and productivity errors are resolved by joint effort among the team. Teams have check points to review all outgoing finished products. Any member of the team can call for group help to reach a consensus on key problems quickly. Feedback mechanisms between each quality circle (QC) team member are immediate. Team members are viewed as teachers and error correction masters.

Principle four: encourage the following quality circle team characteristics

All the members of the team clearly understand and agree on common goals. A forum exists for the sharing of ideas; there is a high level of communication among team members, and everyone participates with enthusiasm. Supervisors or managers support the team to resolve problems when called upon. Reward and recognition are shared among team members.

Principle five: provide clear definitions of roles and responsibilities to the quality circle team

The recommended definitions of roles and responsibilities are as follows:

- *Teacher:* The person who trains team members for the skills needed to perform the task. At one stage or another, everyone on the QC team is a teacher.
- *Team leader:* The person who leads the team through the process of resolving a key problem. The team leader is chosen by voluntary means. Each member of the QC team inherits leadership on a rotational basis.
- *Team members:* A group of people who participate in the problem solving and resolution process. The team meets regularly at specified times at a specified location to provide a consensus that resolves problems related to their tasks.
- *Facilitator:* A team member who records all the team's progress, keeps records of the agenda, and assists the team leader in accomplishing the stated objectives and goals of the QC team.
- *Team correction master:* Any member of the team who identifies a quality error in the output produced by other team members. Such a member ensures that the error is corrected at the source of production or service. All team members participate in a random and revolving inspection process to help detect quality errors.
- *Team presentations:* Presentations to management of team accomplishments are rotated among team members. The presenter introduces team members at the start of the presentation. The agenda and the presentation package are jointly prepared by all members of the team.

The following QER implementation methodology is recommended:

- **Step one:** Allow the formation of the quality circle team to evolve by itself at any level.
- **Step two:** Specific quality circle team formed for a specific problem defines its own set of objectives, agenda, meeting times, procedures and training processes. It is recommended that excessive supervisory and management intervention be avoided at this point.
- **Step three:** Provide the required training for the quality circle team as it relates to specific tasks and decision making processes.

- **Step four:** Train the quality circle team on QER guidelines and principles including problem-solving approaches.
- **Step five:** Quality circle team generates a list of potential problems that require resolution.
- **Step six:** Quality circle team uses Pareto analysis, and cause-and-effect diagrams, to select focus problem(s).
- **Step seven:** Quality circle team brainstorms on the possible root cause of problem. The nominal group technique is recommended at this point.
- **Step eight:** Team analyses problem root causes, develops possible solutions, and reaches consensus on solution implementation strategy and plan.
- **Step nine:** Team prepares progress evaluation procedure and implements new idea(s) to resolve problem.
- **Step ten:** Team presents progress to management periodically, obtains approvals for resources required and specifies action items and benefit dates for implemented action. Team continues to hold regular sessions to follow-up on improvement and look for new areas of opportunity for improvement. The team dissolves when no longer required or there is no meaningful problem for it to resolve.

The use of computers in productivity improvement and statistical process control

Productivity and quality improvement projects often require the gathering and analysis of data on a continuous basis. Collecting data manually is expensive and cumbersome. For example, in a typical high technology manufacturing environment involved in mass production, over 50,000 pieces of data are generated daily on a number of variables and parameters. In such an environment, the manual preparation of tools such as histograms, scatter diagram, control charts and productivity measures is often expensive and difficult. Computers can be invaluable tools in eliminating the difficulty involved in manual data collection and computations. Some of the benefits of using computers as an aid in the decision-making process are as follows:

- They can process large quantities of data quickly, accurately and economically.
- They help to supplement the memories and cognitive limitations of decision-makers.
- They enhance the effectiveness of a decision-maker in both repetitive and non-repetitive tasks involving a considerable amount of information processing, data manipulation and information storage.
- They provide the decision-maker with the ability to communicate faster, and the capability to deal with work pressures and time constraints.

- They provide greater and more efficient computational power needed for trade-off analysis, investment decisions, project design and implementation and manipulating probabilities.
- They provide useful assistance in enhancing various types of cognitive activities, coping with ambiguity, and moving ideas from conceptualisation to implementation.
- They enhance the process of planning, controlling, organising and improving activities in the work environment.
- Computers with efficient software can accurately make complex calculations and complete procedures.

Types of computer system available for productivity improvement and statistical process control

In general, two types of systems are available:

- Single point systems: These are computers developed to support productivity and quality improvement projects through the gathering and analysis of data at a single work station or operational unit. Some of the available single point systems can perform SPC and productivity measurement calculations. A more advanced system can provide graphical display of charts. These systems are available from a whole range of suppliers such as Compag, Dec, IBM, Sigma, Marposs, Mercer, Mitutoyo and AT & T.
- Plant-wide systems: These are computers (mini and mainframes) developed to support specific applications as they relate to data analysis and computations. Most of the available plant-wide systems are efficient and provide the following benefits:
  - Chronological reporting of defects.
  - Variable mapping.
  - Chronological reporting of equipment/tool utilisation.
  - Automatic data collection at the source of production or service.
  - Real time analysis of quality problem.
  - Provision of quick recognition of excessive defect rates.

Several systems are available including Qscan, QDM from Hewlett Packard, Stat PAC from IBM, QDMS from Logica, SPC/SQC from Honeywell and TRACS from Genrad. The Institute of Industrial Engineers, with headquarters at Atlanta, Georgia, publishes periodically a list of available micro and minicomputer packages for productivity and quality improvement.

Introducing computer systems for productivity and quality improvement

The following steps are recommended for introducing computer systems for productivity and quality improvement:

- **Step one:** Perform a thorough review of current operation to evaluate the effectiveness of systems in providing accurate information on improvement projects
- **Step two:** Determine the capability of the existing system or manual method by analysing volume of information, input and output, control points for data tracking and manipulation.
- **Step three:** Develop a need statement for the computer system through a feasibility study and information gathered from steps one and two.
- **Step four:** Identify specific objectives and potential areas of computer systems application.
- **Step five:** Review available systems, test them in real life situations to ensure that the systems will be effective in the particular application being considered.
- **Step six:** Identify the costs, benefits, resource requirements and implementation time-table associated with each system considered. Consider the ratio of multiple users and computing power of all systems considered.
- **Step seven:** Review the flexibility of hardware and software sourcing and how easy it is to develop operating procedures and train potential users of the systems.
- **Step eight:** Select a specific system that meets specifications and requirements, train users, and follow-up periodically on hardware and software updates.

When implemented properly, both single and plant-wide computer systems can serve as effective tools for supplementing the memories and cognitive limitations of decision makers and productivity analysts. The systems can enhance quality, effectiveness and productivity of decision-making behaviour at the source of production or service.

Summary

This section has provided the essential tools for implementing statistical process control, and just-in-time quality improvement tools at the source. Statistical measurement of process variations is required to detect when a process is out of control. Once a process is out of control, the line must be stopped until the assignable causes are fixed. The techniques and tools presented in this section provide a disciplined approach to identifying and solving quality problem and improving productivity at the source. The use of the various tools and techniques presented requires an integrated approach that combines both quantitative and qualitative data and information.

Suggested reading

Braverman, D. Jerome (1981). *Fundamentals of Statistics Quality Control.* Reston Publishing Co. Inc., Virginia.

Deming, Edwards W. (1982). *Productivity, Quality and Competitive Position.* MIT Press, Boston.

Ducan, A. J. (1984). *Quality Control and Industrial Statistics.* Richard D. Irwin, Homewood, Illinois.

Edosomwan, Johnson A. (1986). Statistical process control in group technology production environment. SYNERGY SME Publications.

Edosomwan, Johnson A. (1987). *Integrating Productivity and Quality Management.* Marcel Dekker Inc., New York.

Grant, Eugene I. and Leavenworth, Richard (1972). *Statistical Quality Control,* 4th edn. McGraw-Hill, New York.

Juran, J. M. and Gryna, Frank M. (1980). *Quality Planning and Analysis.* McGraw-Hill, New York.

3 JUST-IN-TIME PRODUCTIVITY ASSESSMENT AND IMPROVEMENT TOOLS

General problem-solving framework

The general problem-solving framework (GPSF) presented in Fig. 3.1 is comprised of a ten-step approach for identifying and resolving production and service problems. Each step is described below:

- **Step one:** Problem identification and objectives clarification. In this step, specific problems are identified by examining the current mode of operation. The use of problem identification tools such as the cause-and-effect diagram, brainstorming techniques and the error removal technique is suggested. The breadth and scope of the problem should be clearly stated. Data from process flow charts, organisation charts, procedures and policies are usually very helpful in specifying the flow of information. Based on the problem(s) identified, specific objectives are formulated. These objectives provide a basis for solution and evaluation.

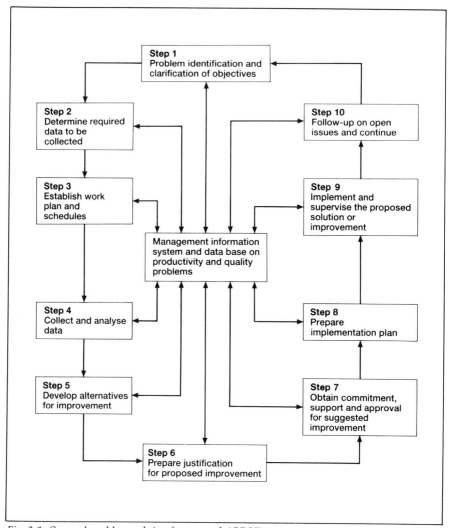

Fig. 3.1 General problem solving framework (GPSF).

- **Step two:** Determine data to be collected. This is usually accomplished through understanding the existing methods of accomplishing tasks. The scope of the problem(s) identified in the first step determines how many data are to be collected.

- **Step three:** Establish work plan and schedules. It is recommended that the overall problem identified in the first step be broken down into smaller units by tasks and key processes. This will facilitate the analysis of all segments of the problem. Prepare plan for addressing the problem with specific detailed work schedule, including distribution of activities to be accomplished to individuals and departments which have responsibility for resolution.

- **Step four:** Collect and analyse data. Ensure that the source of data for the problems being addressed is adequate. Carefully observe the activity under analysis to be sure it is thoroughly understood. Analysing the data requires attention to the following details:

- Data classification.
- Data verification.
- Data synthesis.
- Checking tables, weights, figures.
- Error verification.

- **Step five:** Develop alternatives for improvement. Re-examine the problem(s) identified in the first step and evaluate the effect of anticipated changes. Collect ideas for solving the problem(s) and improving the situation and make preliminary plans for proposed improvement.
- **Step six:** Prepare justification for the proposed improvement with emphasis on the following:

  - Cost impact assessment.
  - Capital investment.
  - Rate of return.
  - Intangible benefits.
  - Productivity and quality benefits.

- **Step seven:** Obtain commitment, support and approval for suggested improvement. Review the proposed improvement with both management and employees affected by the change. Revise improvement alternatives based on their input.
- **Step eight:** Prepare implementation plan. The implementation plan should include activities, individual responsibilities and time frame.
- **Step nine:** Implement the proposed solution and supervise the installation for effectiveness. The implementation process should include the training of personnel in proposed changes, resource allocation and balancing.
- **Step ten:** Follow up on open issues and continue to focus on continuous improvement. Watch closely for erratic changes, perform periodic evaluation of what has been accomplished and continue to seek new improvement opportunities.

Process management

Process management involves a systematic approach for understanding the boundaries, conditions and interdependencies between the input and output of operational units, tasks, departments, suppliers, customers and organisation. The components and characteristics of a typical process is shown systematically in Fig. 3.2. The major differences between a manufacturing and service process are also presented in Table 3.1. The techniques recommended for process analysis are detailed below.

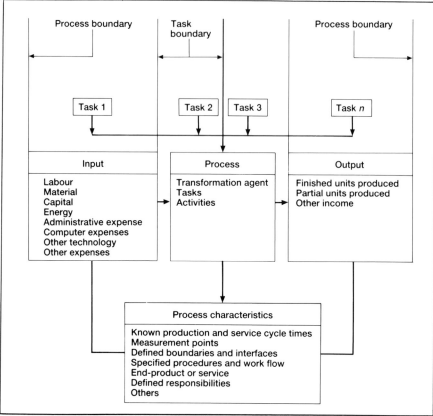

Fig. 3.2 The components and characteristics of a typical process.

Table 3.1 Elements of process management in manufacturing and service environments

Element	Manufacturing sector	Service sector
Measurement	Defined quantitative measures	Partially quantitative and highly quantitative
Inputs	Highly tangible	Both tangible and intangible
Outputs	Highly tangible	Both tangible and intangible
Ownership	Easy to define	Difficult to define. High level of ambiguity exists
Boundaries	Easy to define	May be unclear in most situations
Interfaces	Easy to define	May be unclear in some situations
Control	Well established	Partially in existence
Corrective action	Has defined procedure	Defined and reactive procedure
Productivity and quality measures	Highly defined	Partially defined
Value systems	Mostly tangible	Mostly intangible
Process cycle times	Well defined	Partially defined
Process characteristics	Repetitive tasks Very common product-oriented technologies	Non-repetitive tasks very common Service-oriented technologies
Customer base	Well defined	Partially defined
Supplier base	Well defined	Well defined

Input–output analysis technique

The input–output technique is a systematic approach to outlining and defining the specific detailed activities within the input, process and output of each task or operational unit. This approach combines knowledge of work processes and interviews with employees to identify specific bottlenecks affecting the inputs, process and outputs. The following steps are recommended for performing input–output analysis.

- **Step one:** Understand all the deliverables within each task. Each element required to satisfy the task activities must be analysed separately, and there must be specific focus on reliability of inputs, process, required quantity, cost, delivery times, and source. A careful analysis of the various inputs (labour, material, energy, capital, technology, etc.) can provide the basis for minimising the cost of production, and reducing defect levels and the cost of quality.
- **Step two:** Analyse each process step and activity for potential errors. In this step the activities required to satisfy the output are analysed. Specific attention is focused on process logistics, boundaries, communication channels, added value of each process step, effectiveness of each process step, process controls and measures.
- **Step three:** Seek improvement ideas. After the input and output elements of each task have been defined, specific ideas that could improve performance should be developed. The ideas can be obtained from process owners, productivity and quality improvement analysts or through a brainstorming approach.
- **Step four:** Implement process improvement ideas and follow-up on open items. In this step, specific improvement ideas identified in each area are implemented by process owners and other individuals charged with responsibility. Follow up and measure performance of the new improvement action(s).

Process analysis technique (PAT)

This is a systematic approach to defining all tasks required to execute a process. The following steps are recommended for performing the PAT:

- **Step one:** Select a particular process based on the degree of productivity and quality problem.
- **Step two:** List the value added and non-value added task within the process.
- **Step three:** Record process times for all activities.
- **Step four:** Based on the information obtained in steps two and three, determine which task or activity is required to produce the final output.
- **Step five:** Seek alternative approaches or methods to perform existing task at reduced cost and improved quality levels.

- **Step six:** Eliminate the waste and non-value added tasks and implement improved value added methods in the process.
- **Step seven:** Implement the right controls for process monitoring and follow-up on continuous improvement actions.

Task simplification and work flow analysis

Task simplification and work flow analysis involves a step-by-step approach to investigating and analysing contemplated and present task and work systems, methods and procedures for the purpose of developing easier, quicker, less fatiguing and more economical ways of providing high quality goods and services. The following steps are recommended for conducting task simplification and work flow analysis:

- **Step one:** Identify the specific task and work flow pattern that needs improvement. Clearly define the purpose, objectives, start and end points of process tasks. This can be accomplished by drawing the flow chart of the particular process with recorded processing time.
- **Step two:** Analyse the task process and work flow pattern for improvement. Focus specifically on duplication of activities, effort, resources, bottle-necks, excessive transportation and delays.
- **Step three:** Eliminate process bottle-necks and duplication of activities and implement an improved process and work flow pattern. Follow up on implemented actions with continuous improvement efforts.

The nominal group technique

The nominal group technique (NGT) is a pro-active search process that involves a participative group approach in identifying specific production and service problems and issues, providing ideas and solutions to resolve the problems identified. NGT provides the forum for all members of the group to participate in problem identification, solution selection and ranking. The following steps shown in Fig. 3.3 are recommended for conducting NGT:

- **Step one:** Idea generation process. In this step, the leader of the group presents the purpose of the meeting and lists specific productivity and quality problems. The ground rules for group participation are also provided.
- **Step two:** Round robin silent reporting of ideas. Participants present new ideas and they are recorded. All ideas are reported as presented with each person contributing an idea in turn and no evaluation and prejudgment permitted. The leader of the group can also participate in providing his or her own ideas.
- **Step three:** Clarification of ideas and group discussions. All the ideas presented are discussed to ensure that there is group consensus on the

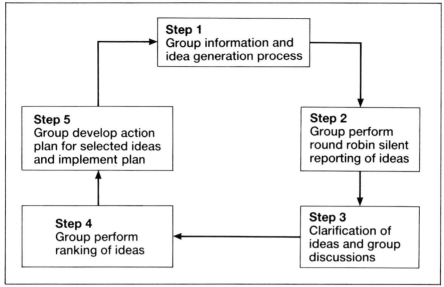

Fig. 3.3 Nominal group technique (NGT) implementation steps.

main ideas provided. Some of the ideas are combined in a logical manner.

- **Step four:** Brainstorm on possible alternatives and ranking of ideas. In this step, all participants rank each idea in order of priority and select three to five top priority ideas. Each ranking is recorded by the group leader as presented. Consensus is reached by the group on the first three priority ideas.
- **Step five:** The group works together to develop an implementation plan and establish a benefit date for each idea selected.

Value analysis approach

The value analysis is a systematic approach to examining the functional design of a product or specific part, to develop a more efficient, less costly alternative. The following steps are recommended for implementing the value analysis approach:

- **Step one:** Select the product or part for analysis and evaluate its importance.
- **Step two:** Develop functional definition of the part and describe its purpose and use in the product in question. Specific questions to ask when analysing parts are:
  - Does it contribute to the use of the product?
  - Is it cost effective?
  - Are all the features required?
  - Are there alternative parts that are better?

- Can recycled material be used?
- Can another supplier provide the part for less cost?
- Can the function of the part be combined with something else?

- **Step three:** Collect data on part performance and cost and evaluate the contribution of the part to the final product.
- **Step four:** Develop alternatives. Conduct a brainstorming session to determine its function and to develop ways to overcome any apparent road-blocks.
- **Step five:** Design or establish specifications for the proposed new component or part.
- **Step six:** Evaluate the new part through prototype testing and compare the cost of new and existing parts. Select the best alternative.
- **Step seven:** Implement the preferred part in the product design and subassembly and put it into operation. Follow-up to ascertain that the new part is performing the same function at a lower cost and improved quality.

Just-in-time technique

Just-in-time technique defined

Just-in-time (JIT) is an integrated disciplined process management approach that uses teamwork and the pull control system to improve productivity and quality at the source through enforced problem solving, and the elimination of waste and defects, process bottle-necks and barriers, and uses proper planning and scheduling of total production and service requirements to reduce inventory and process cycle times. The teamwork approach encompasses maximum cooperation between the supplier, producer and process owners as well as strong commitment from both management and employee to providing the right material at the right place, at the right time, and doing the job right the first time at the source. Fig. 3.4 presents the elements involved in managing JIT total requirements. The elements must be managed continuously with emphasis on product and process simplification, set up reductions, preventative actions in place for defects and problem solving tools utilised for error cause removal.

Just-in-time benefits

JIT applications in a production environment can offer the following benefits:

- Improved productivity and quality at the source through enforced problem solving and error cause removal.

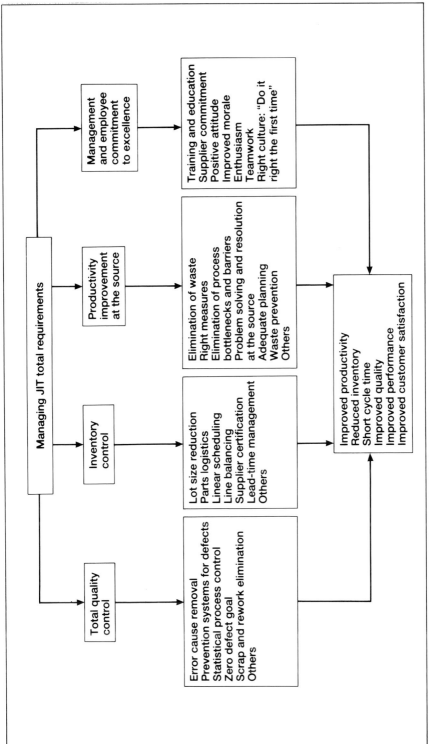

Fig. 3.4 Elements involved in managing JIT total requirements.

- Reduction in the amount of work-in-process (WIP) and overall inventory levels, with a better and increased inventory turnover ratio.
- Increased process flexibility and ability to respond to customer requirements.
- Reduced space requirement, cost of quality and overheads.
- Reduced process cycle times and lead-time for procurement of parts and materials.
- Improved employee morale through the elimination of waste, process bottle-necks and barriers that hinder productivity and quality improvement.
- Reduced set-up times and material handling.
- Quick visibility of production problems.
- Elimination of parts shortages and stabilisation of production schedules.

Just-in-time implementation steps

The following JIT implementation steps are recommended:

- **Step one:** Obtain commitment from management and employee through education and training. In this step, education and training of both management and employees on the JIT concept is recommended. The training should focus on the benefits, tools and JIT principles and requirements. If done correctly, JIT education and training should help establish the right culture and commitment to the discipline required for JIT implementation. Such commitment includes doing the job right at the source of production or service, with a realistic and achievable zero defect goal. Inventory is an unwanted evil, and customer satisfaction demands the right goods and services at the right place, with the right content and at the right time.
- **Step two:** Establish a pilot project team. The JIT pilot project team should comprise of representatives from all functional areas. The team establishes JIT goals and objectives as well as identifying and prioritising areas for potential improvements. The improvement opportunities usually cover, but are not limited to, the following areas: process simplification, elimination of waste, reduction in lot size and lead-time, inventory reduction, rework and scrap, parts and material pipeline management.
- **Step three:** Select specific production sector for a pilot project to implement JIT techniques and establish key requirements. In this step, the project team focuses on a particular sector of the production environment to begin implementation of the JIT technique. However, the following requirements must be developed and executed:
  - Construct and implement the right production or service cells or Kanbans. The cells or Kanbans provide an organised and systematic approach for regulating the flow of material, product and services.

They are tied together by a process information network that regulates the plant-wide production flow.

- Identify areas for improvement within each cell. This requires evaluation of process flow analysis, development of flowcharts, estimating process cycle time, simulating the line to see if the process is balanced evaluating incoming parts and setup requirement.
- Identify yields and specific improvement alternatives and actions. Identify sources of errors and prioritise problems using Pareto analysis, matrix analysis technique and nominal group technique.

- **Step four:** Implement actions to address specific problem areas. Usually the following areas require attention.

  - *Total Quality Control.* The defects and errors generated within a specific process can be eliminated by implementing statistical process control (SPC) techniques. SPC is an effective technique for understanding process variation through quantifiable data and, by taking corrective action through analysis of assignable causes, process defects can be eliminated. The following techniques are recommended for SPC: cause-and-effect diagram (fish-bone diagram), histograms, control charts, Pareto analyses, design of experiment and variable mapping techniques. The strategy to eliminate defects should also include providing the right training for employees, providing the right tools and techniques and the decision latitude that enables everyone to have control over his own areas of responsibility.
  - *Productivity Improvement through Work Simplification.* This can be accomplished through an ongoing process of improvement. Continuous improvement comes from dedicated team effort that constantly evaluates the current ways of doing things and through organised use of common sense, implement better methods and techniques to improve overall performance. The general problem solving framework recommended for continuous problem analysis and improvement has been presented in Fig. 3.1. The areas to focus on are: process simplification, distribution of work, operations analysis, delays, excessive transportation, lead-time reduction and cross-functional barriers.
  - *Production and Service Requirements Planning.* Successful implementation of JIT also requires an organised approach for planning the total production and service requirements. The planning mechanism should be able to provide a base for periodic assessment of demand, capacity analysis, lead-time between orders, backlog control, and daily scheduling of parts and materials through each cell Kanban. Several techniques are available: materials requirement planning, parts frozen zone management, master production schedule control. What is required is the appropriate planning tool that coordinates demand statement with build quantity to ensure that the right goods and services are delivered at the right place, at the right time, in the

right amount. Usually through appropriate supply-chain management the implementation of the right production and service planning techniques can be achieved. Adequate supply-chain management requires focus on vendor selection and certification, vendor process control, vendor audit and ongoing communication between vendor and producers on key supply issues as they relate to parts, materials and services expected. The following steps are recommended for inventory control:

- Classify all parts and materials by unit costs.
- Complete the periodic demand for each item using the economic order quantity formula:

$$EOQ = \sqrt{\frac{2A_u O_s}{I_c U_c}}$$

where A_u = annual usage for a specific part or material, O_s = set-up or ordering cost, I_c = inventory carrying cost, U_c = unit cost for each item or material.

- Prioritise all items using unit cost and classify all items by ABC code.
- Establish certified vendors for each item. Establish purchase orders and agreement for delivery items by pull system. Establish minimum order quantity and safety stock required for just-in-time production.
- Establish inventory control policy and code for each item and monitor inventory performance periodically.

As shown in Fig. 3.5, successful JIT implementation also requires attention to all production boundaries. The 6C principles of co-operation, communication, cost avoidance, controls, contribution analysis and coordination are recommended for improving the performance of all production boundaries. On-going evaluation and improvement is required within each cell and the total system boundaries. The process owner must discuss and share capacity plans with the supplier and they must work together to ensure that defect-free products are supplied.

- *Preventative Maintenance and Error Environment.* JIT requires routine maintenance of tools, equipment and processes to be done periodically. First, the process and task environment must be organised adequately to provide visibility to potential production and service problems. An organised and clean environment stimulates improvement in productivity and quality. A hazard-free work environment should be provided for all employees, the work layout, process design tools, equipment and other facilities should be evaluated periodically for improvement.

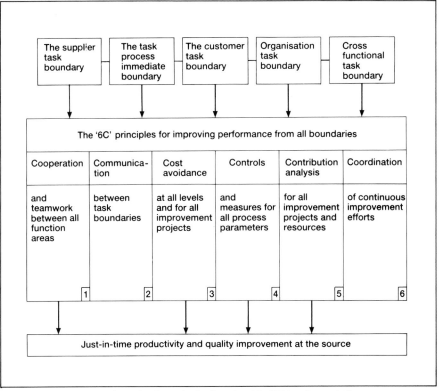

Fig.3.5 Production and service boundaries involved in JIT implementation.

- **Step five:** Expand the use of the JIT technique to other production sectors and focus on continuous improvement. Improving productivity and quality through JIT applications requires ongoing improvement efforts in materials management, product logistics, product and process simplification, elimination of waste and defects. JIT is a disciplined approach that continually seeks higher levels of improvement in managing the interrelations between production and service systems.
- **Step Six:** Measure results and take corrective action. Table 3.2 provide JIT requirements and self assessment checklist recommended for monitoring the effectiveness of a specific JIT project or programme. The idea is to capitalise on the success factors and areas, and to identify sources of failure and weaknesses and fix them.

Phasing technique for just-in-time material flow process

In constructing JIT materials flow process, the four phases presented in Fig. 3.6 is recommended. These are process analysis and preparatory phase, classification of Kanbans and parts disbursement, preparation for vendor direct shipment, and vendor direct delivery of parts to the manufacturing line.

Table 3.2 JIT requirements and self assessment checklist

	Rating			Action	Benefit date for completed
Requirements	Excellent	Good	Poor	plan	actions
Continuous flow for all parts					
Common process					
Certified vendors					
Scrap rate defined					
Controlled production					
One way flow for materials					
No staging areas					
Problem-solving tools					
Reduced set-up times					
Total quality control					
Reduced cycle time					
Production logistics					
Inventory control defined					
Employee and management involvement in problem resolution					
Inspection procedure defined					
Minimise process variance					
Material queues					
Preventative maintenance					
Supplier-chain management					
Process measurements in place					
Zero safety stock					
Eliminate kiting					
Pull system for material					
Continuous work flow analysis					
Good housekeeping					
Minimum lot size					
Zero waiting time					
Zero work-in-process					
Standardisation of product					
Standardisation of process					
Dedicated work cell					
Dedicated equipment					
Others					

Phase one. Process analysis and preparation

This phase concerns itself with reviewing the task ahead. It is apparent that streamlining the materials flow process is not easy. Therefore, a team must be formed to encompass diverse disciplines. This team requires resources from various areas including industrial engineering, manufacturing engineering, production control, systems engineering, supplier quality engineering, supplier manufacturing engineering and procurement/ purchasing. A long lead-time for design and implementation is essential. This process, although consistent in many steps, will vary with product type, parts, and, primarily, from a new product to an already established, manufactured product. With an already established product, the vendors, delivery habits, warehouse procedures, and packaging have previously

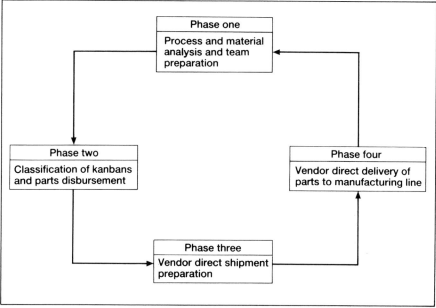

Fig. 3.6 Four phase approach for JIT material flow process.

been established; therefore, extra effort may be required to change these prehistoric concepts and processes of parts distribution.

Part prioritisation. Initially, a pre-design feasibility analysis must be performed by the team. This analysis begins with an intensive definition of the parts. A matrix is formed consisting of data compiled on the type of parts, usage, historical quality of each part, packaging quantities, and vendor origin of each part. The matrix configuration will be very efficient in performing various data references. This matrix can then be utilised to construct a priority list of parts targeted for direct shipment from the vendor to the manufacturing line. Prioritisation of a part can be based on size, cost, usage, quality, vendor service level, and other elements that impact on space and cost. Weighted numbers are then applied to each of these elements, relating to their importance (i.e., if the facility is limited on space allocation, space may be given a factor of 10, on a 1–10 scale). Next, each part number is given a rating factor for each element. One method of rating may be performed by classifying the parts into space categories (i.e., parts in the 10–20 sq. feet requirement are given a 10, 5–9 sq. feet are given a 9, etc.). This methodology is then applied to the remaining elements and part numbers to construct a matrix. One column can be used for the summation of the particular part number weighted number. The matrix should then show the prioritisation for 'direct ship' candidates, with those having a higher weighted number given the higher priority. As is apparent in the matrix displayed in Table 3.3, part number Z is obviously a lower priority direct ship candidate with an index factor of 135; however, part number X, with an index factor of 432, is a highly attractive direct ship candidate. Part number X would be targeted for immediate direct shipping. A LOTUS spreadsheet

Table 3.3 Parts prioritisation matrix

Weighted numbers used to derive index factors	--	9	9	10	10	10	10
Part number	Usage	Size	Cost unit	Carrying cost	Vendor service	Quality level	Index factor
X	2	9	9	9	8	10	432
Y	3	7	4	4	2	1	169
Z	1	3	2	2	3	4	135

is very effective in the compilation of the matrix with computations to multiply the element by the rating factor for each part number and summing these totals to derive an index factor.

Small parts, such as screws, nuts, and bolts or other high volume/low cost parts should not be included in the matrix. These parts can be handled in a min/max type of system. A 'breadman' concept can be applied to these parts, with the operator ordering and supplying these parts versus the material handler. The matrix should then be reviewed to construct a Gantt chart of which parts should be direct shipped immediately and when, and which parts should be phased in for direct shipment. An example is shown in Table 3.4.

Another matrix or an enhancement to the original one, can now be constructed to include the listing of parts with corresponding vendors, time of day, day(s) of the week, and packaging quantities and a proposed delivery schedule, based on the parts prioritisation matrix, can be derived. This analysis is essential to ensure that dock and manufacturing space capacity is not exceeded and to avoid bottle-necks at the incoming parts area. A simulation of this process is extremely useful in constructing a schedule of numerous vendors.

The parts matrix can then be formatted to yield disbursement locations. Each part is given an alphanumeric code to correspond with a location of final destination, where it will be used. This code can be a bar-code label, placed on the packaging and part at the vendor, acknowledged in the system upon receipt, when the part is placed in the corresponding warehouse location, and forwarded to the corresponding location of the manufacturing process routing to a designated manufacturing cell. This design will allow for initial phase requirements as well as full implementation provisions. These locations should be incorporated into all layouts.

Table 3.4 Typical Gantt chart for parts direct shipment

Part number	Vendor	1Q88	2Q88	3Q88	4Q88	1Q89	2Q89
X	ABC CO.	W----	D----	----	----	----	----
Y	UNITED	BW----	W----	D----	----	----	----
Z	DEF INC.	M----	BW----	W----	D----	----	----

M-Monthly,   BW-Bi-Weekly,   D-Daily/Direct Ship

The matrices can now be used by independent committees of the team. The system group, along with production control group can determine if existing material requirements planning (MRP) programmes can handle the proposed ordering and delivery methods; provisions should be made to ensure consistency at the vendor. Also, the vendor will eventually require a system to allow for full serviceability, visibility to schedules and demand, as well as depletion of parts. The supplier quality engineering and procurement/purchasing should pursue the vendor relation aspect to determine co-operation from various vendors. Vendor contracts will prove essential to gain commitment to stringent delivery and quality standards, as well as incorporating new packaging designs into existing processes. Supplier manufacturing should examine the parts that can be pre-assembled at the vendor. Industrial engineering, manufacturing engineering and production control departments should derive all workload associated with the project, and should define new job descriptions.

The industrial engineering group must now construct a detailed layout to reflect specific space and layout designs to incorporate the strategy and location of parts. This layout must show the transgression from the present to the future in a phase diagram.

With the completion of the above steps, the team may now approach the phasing process. The phasing process consists of the following: implementation of initial concepts in the internal facility while preparing for the next phase, which reduces inventory and begins direct shipping towards a full blown implementation of full vendor serviceability achieved. These phases are based on an already existing process utilising a warehouse. The key achievements of the phase process is elimination of the warehouse and provision of a full vendor service. Focus items are operator ownership, elimination of work effort, and elimination of space. Although each phase focuses on reduction of inventory, beginning with two weeks going to one, a more sophisticated system as a base may prove an expedited implementation and the phase requirements may be altered, depending on the particular application. This process only serves as a model.

Phase two. Classification of kanbans and parts disbursement

Phase two implementation focuses on three objectives.

- Definition of parts Kanbans.
- Disbursing parts to Kanban and manufacturing locations.
- Incorporating small parts in one location in a min/max operation with manufacturing ownership.

The concentration in phase two is to implement initial concepts internally in the manufacturing facility. If a warehouse is used, it can still be maintained in phase two however, it should now be disbursing parts to a particular location or manufacturing cell.

The parts Kanban represents parts supply to meet production demand for one week. This quantity varies from week to week in proportion to demand, but the space allocated is based on the highest weekly volume forecast within the phase two time frame which will be dependent upon the time frame feasible for direct shipping the first set of prioritised direct ship part numbers, determined from the review of the matrix. Based on the particular application, one or two-week Kanban strategy can be applied. If quality and part shortage reaction time is not sufficient to begin with one Kanban, two identical Kanbans can be constructed, thus providing two-week reaction and delivery time. While one Kanban is depleting, the second can be filling. The Kanbans should be designed to separate manufacturing cells or disbursement locations, with bins or shelves to reflect the part number and quantity used. These locations are also consistent with cells on the manufacturing floor.

Internally, the parts may flow from a dock, where acknowledgment occurs, then into the Kanban, then onto the manufacturing floor, providing a two-week cycle time of parts distribution.

To introduce operator ownership, the manufacturing operators can design corresponding parts Kanbans at their stations with colour-coded locations corresponding in the cell.

Externally, the parts would flow from the vendor suppliers to the warehouse, to the facility dock, drop area, into the second Kanban, then classified as the first Kanban (when one week from production), then into the corresponding assembly cell.

The key indicators in phase two are quality, part shortages, and integrity of the parts being disbursed to the correct location. Various statistical charts can be used to perform measurement of these indicators to determine the feasibility of phase three.

Simultaneously with this measurement process, various vendor negotiations are underway to provide for direct shipment of parts to the line. When these measurements indicate that the quality of parts and delivery is sufficient, the Kanban will be reduced to one week or one Kanban.

Phase three. Preparation for vendor direct shipment

The objectives of phase three are to prepare for vendors for direct shipment through implementation of a semi JIT delivery, reducing the delivery time from two weeks' shipment to one week, and eventually to one day in phase four, full implementation. In phase three, the first set of direct ship parts should be direct shipped from the vendor. The remaining parts can be delivered in a semi JIT manner, shipped in one-week quantities versus two. Also, in this phase the internal facility will be operating from one Kanban only. Simultaneously with these operations, the vendors should be qualified from a quality and delivery standpoint to become JIT vendors. Also, in this phase, the various parts that are delivered from the same vendor and utilised in the same process should be designed to be pre-assembled at the vendor, thus reducing cycle time, manpower, and cost.

The warehouse should now be reduced to provide only the services of a distribution centre. The distribution centre would only store the parts; this still provides a buffer against parts shortages until the vendor yields proof of a daily serviceability, but provides significant reduction (one week's worth of inventory) over phase two.

After successful implementation of phase three, completion of vendor and operator training, and contracts signed, phase four can be approached.

Phase four. Vendor direct delivery of parts to the manufacturing line

Phase four shows the implementation of a fully streamlined materials flow for a JIT system. It should provide for a full service, vendor-targeted for direct delivery to the manufacturing line on a daily basis, with no Kanbans, and complete ownership of parts control by the manufacturing operator. The parts should flow from the vendor to the manufacturing location where they are used.

Production and service improvement technique (PASIT)

The production and service improvement technique (PASIT) is a disciplined process improvement approach that requires on-going process assessment and organised use of common sense to find easier and better ways of doing work and streamlining the production and service processes to ensure that goods and services are offered at minimum cost. The PASIT concept is present in Fig. 3.7. The PASIT improvement strategy focuses on the following areas:

- Elimination of bottle-necks.
- Reduction in production cost.
- Reduction in wasted materials.
- Reduction in engineering changes.
- Reduction in non-value added operations.
- Reduction of the amount of paper work.
- Reduction in chronic overtime.
- Reduction in error rate.
- Reduction in work repetition.
- Reduction in work-in-process inventory.
- Reduction in transportation and materials handling.
- Reduction in training time.
- Improved job safety.
- Improved employee morale.
- Improved customer service.
- Improved productivity and quality at the source.

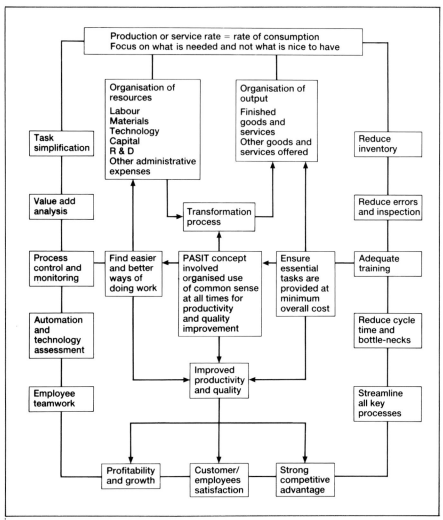

Fig. 3.7 PASIT conceptual framework.

The PASIT principles are as follows:

Principle 1

Management and employees must have the positive attitude that productivity and quality improvement can result from the organised use of common sense to address service and production problems. Management support must be shown through example, practice and an organisation policy statement.

Principle 2

A total teamwork approach among functional organisations, such as research and development, marketing, personnel, purchasing, manufactur-

ing, information systems, quality, facilities and distribution, maintenance, finance, production control, service centres, engineering, and others,
must be used to address all problems.

Principle 3

There must be total productivity and quality improvement at the source of
production or service. Heavy reliance on inspection and other non-value
adding operations within the work organisation must be discouraged. The
required basic training must be provided to obtain good quality goods and
services at the source of production or service.

Principle 4

Reduction in the layers of management at all levels must be encouraged.
Ownership must be given to those charged with task responsibility, and
they must have the control and support needed to resolve daily service and
production problems. Too many levels of management cause additional
bottle-necks. A level of management must be instituted within the organisation only if it will provide value adding to the improvement of the production and service function.

Principle 5

There must be total impact assessment for all service and process changes,
policy changes, and implementation of new ideas and techniques. The new
process, service, ideas, organisation, or management must be better than
the one it replaces, considering all implications.

Principle 6

A total reward system, based on contribution to improving and managing
all aspects of a task to obtain acceptable goods and services, must be in
place. There must be pay for performance in total technical and people
management, and a crisis loop reward system that affects the morale of the
employees must be avoided.

Principle 7

Production and service errors that affect productivity and quality are con-
trollable through common sense and good judgement. The production rate
must be equal to the consumption rate.

Principle 8

Both management and employees must be encouraged to question every
task and job in detail. The ability to wonder about the way tasks are performed, to question each step of the task, the power to generalise problems
areas and solution strategies and the capacity to apply solutions to fix the
obvious problems must be available.

Principle 9

Both management and employees must be encouraged to eliminate unwanted processes and procedures, to combine work elements to reduce waste and repetition, to have the courage to change the sequence of events if this leads to improvement and continually to simplify work processes.

Principle 10

Both management and employees should adopt the practice of seeing every job as make ready, do it and put it away.

PASIT implementation steps

The following steps are recommended for implementing PASIT:

- **Step one:** Establish a PASIT team that is made up of representatives from all functional areas. The team member must possess through training the ability to resolve problems quickly.
- **Step two:** Train the team on PASIT principles and concepts including problem-solving techniques.
- **Step three:** Let the PASIT team select a pilot project for improvement. The project selection is done after a thorough analysis of problem areas and prioritisation of impact and potential benefits to be derived when a new method is implemented.
- **Step four:** The PASIT team reviews operational parameters to understand the current situation. This requires six basis steps:

    - Orientation to people, processes, and procedures.
    - Information gathering.
    - Interviewing.
    - Preparing work distribution charts.
    - Preparing process flow charts.
    - Developing task elements lists.

    This step should focus on the detailed review of tasks performed by individuals, work groups, departments, and functions, the methods used; and the flow of work from one task to another and among the members of the work group. It is also important to identify the volume of work and the frequency, rate, and timing involved in each task performed. In order to ensure adequate coverage of all key information, it is important to have a data-gathering checklist similar to that shown in Table 3.2.
    Orientation. The orientation phase enables the analyst to know all the key processes, procedures, and people in the various organisations. The functions for each work group must be clearly understood. Attention must also be paid to interfunctional dependencies. The objective is to get all facts on the task performed by asking ten basic questions:

- What is it?
- What does it do?
- Who does it?
- What does it cost?
- Where is it being done?
- What is it worth?
- When is it done?
- Why is it done?
- Who has the authority to say so?
- Who has ownership for it?

The interviewing process should be structured to obtain an opinion from every level of employee and management. The important point is to ensure that the analyst works with facts, not opinions. A scheduled time for interviews by a random selection process should also be encouraged.

Work distribution charts, process charts, and task elements. Work distribution charts, process flowcharts, and task element recording formats are organised ways of recording the information gathered from questionnaires, interviews, and process procedures. These charts enable analysts to identify the various task activities to be measured and to estimate the time spent by each individual or work group on each task. Flowcharts show the sequence of steps required to perform a task. Flowcharts also provide the basis for understanding the relationship between the task and the processing times. Task elements enable analysts to determine the extent of skill utilisation, work specialisation, delays, transportation required, and other details necessary to pinpoint and understand the process parameters.

- **Step five:** Perform operation analysis of selected focus problem(s) in performing an operations analysis of a selected pilot project. The following information is required:

  - Develop task flow diagram.
  - Record the processing times for each task.
  - Record setup time for each task.
  - Identify all transportation logistical data.
  - Simulate the parameters to understand input and output from each sector and leverage area. Simulation also identifies the impact of changes in processing times on other parameters.

  The analysis of the information specified above provides the basis to determine bottle-necks, rework loops, capacity limitation and resource constraints. Table 3.5 summarises the four major questions that need to be answered and the expected results.
- **Step six:** Analyse current operations to determine the magnitude of problems identified. The feasibility and suitability of all parameters should be determined based on cost, value added, time, and impact on quality. Other factors to consider are: work safety, job satisfaction and employee morale.

Table 3.5 PASIT operation analysis questions and results

Question	Result
Who is performing the task?	Reveals hidden organisational problems
	Shows division of responsibility and improvement
	Use of authority and potential improvements
	Communications problems and potential improvements
	Skill base and experiences
	Level of authority and decision making power
	Technical vitality
What task is done?	Redistribution of task
	Elimination of waste and unnecessary task
	Proper utilisation of skills
	Consolidation of group activities
	Elimination of wasted efforts
	Balancing of group tasks
	Balancing of input and output rate for each sector
	Correct skill deficiencies
	Task dependencies
	Time utilisation
How is the task done?	Simplification of tasks
	Prioritisation of task elements
	Elimination of excessive delays and transportation
	Rearrangement of work stations
	Use of faster methods or tools
	Changes in processing time
	Work load balancing
	Performance assessment
Where is the task done?	Scrapping unwanted tools and equipment
	Efficient location of work stations
	Elimination of unwanted transportation
	Improvement in morale of employees
	Reduced design hazards at work stations
	Changes in ergonomic arrangements
	Changes in work design
	Changes in tool design
	Changes in task sequence

- **Step seven:** Analyse each task for improvement: six approaches, presented below, are recommended for operations and service improvement.

    - Eliminate and minimise the number of task elements within a given operation.
    - Maximise the use of all resources available.
    - Combine and rearrange the sequences of processes.
    - Substitute and simplify methods of performing a given task.
    - Change the sequence for performing a given task.
    - Use a new technology or tool to replace the method of performing a given task.

- **Step eight:** Implement the new methods and techniques and evaluate their effectiveness. The teamwork approach should be used for implementation to minimise resistance to change. The evaluation of the new method or technique should be done using the following criteria:

  - Cost and savings related to the specific alternative.
  - Quality improvement related to the specific alternative.
  - Job satisfaction and morale improvement related to the special alternative.
  - Capability of the user to adapt to the specific alternative.
  - Implementation requirements of the specific alternative.
  - Time required to meet all objectives specified in the specific alternative.
  - Conformation of the specific alternative to established policy and standards.
  - Specific known exposures related to a specific alternative.
  - Justification of new alternative tools using the total productivity measurement approach.
  - Justification of a new alternative using cost-benefit analysis and other financial measures.
  - Total investment required to implement the new method or technique.

  Use managerial judgement to assess the degree of tangible and intangible benefits.

- **Step nine:** Follow up on open issues and focus on continuous improvement in all sectors of the production and service environment.

Productivity measurement

The task-oriented total productivity measurement model (TOTPM) is recommended for assessing total, total factor and partial productivities. The following basic definitions associated with the model are provided.

Task

A task is a unit of work accomplished primarily at a single location (site), by a single agent, during a single time period, producing useful output from some resources available.

Total productivity

Total productivity is the ratio of total measurable output, total finished units produced, partial units produced, or other income or output associated with units produced to the sum of all the measurable inputs (labour, materials, capital, energy, robotics, computers, other technology, data-processing and other administrative expenses) utilised for production or service.

Total factor productivity

Total factor productivity is the ratio of total measurable output to the sum of labour and capital inputs.

Partial productivity

This is the ratio of total measurable output to one class of measurable input (for example, materials utilised for production).

Implementation steps for the task-oriented total productivity measurement model

In Table 3.6 the input and output elements of the TOTPM are presented with the expressions for computing total, total factor and partial productivities. The following steps are recommended for implementing the TOTPM:

Table 3.6 Input and output elements of TOTPM

Measurable ouputs
Finished units produced
Partial units produced
Other income associated with units produced
Dividends and interest associated with units produced

Measurable inputs
Labour
Material
Capital
Energy
Computers
Research and development
Robotics
Other technology
Other expenses
Data processing
Administrative expenses
Miscellaneous expenses

$$\text{Total productivity} = \frac{\textit{Total measurable output in constant monetary value}}{\textit{Total measurable input in constant monetary terms}}$$

$$\text{Total factor productivity} = \frac{\textit{Total measurable output in constant monetary value}}{\textit{Total measurable value of capital and labour input in constant monetary terms}}$$

$$\text{Partial productivity} = \frac{\textit{Total measurable output in constant monetary value}}{\textit{Measurable value of one input in constant monetary terms}}$$

- **Step one:** Understand the various products and services including the process and resources utilised for production of goods and services. Become familiar with all key personnel to understand who does what and how. Understand the various inputs and outputs and the transformation process used to process inputs and record the value of each input and output element.
- **Step two:** Perform sales, cost and project analysis on all products and services rendered. Use Pareto analysis to select the vital few for productivity measurement focus.
- **Step three:** Develop allocation criteria for all the input and output components. The proportional contributions to sales is often used for output allocation. The proportional contribution to total finished and partial units produced, insertion rate, energy rate, and floor space consumed are often used for allocation of input elements.
- **Step four:** Design a data collection system to capture the input and output elements in monetary value.
- **Step five:** Select a base period for productivity comparison. A base period is a reference period to which the productivity values are compared to obtain productivity indices. The base period should be a normal period where there is no unusual activity within the production or service processes.
- **Step six:** Use consumer price indexes to generate deflators. Deflators are used to reduce the monetary values of input and output to constant monetary values. The deflators ensure that the productivity values and indices are not based on inflationary monetary values.
- **Step seven:** Collect data on input and output elements periodically and record areas for improvement.
- **Step eight:** Synthesise the data collected to ensure they are representative of the input and output elements.
- **Step nine:** Compute productivity values and indices periodically by using the definition of total, total factor and partial productivities.
- **Step ten:** Plot the productivity values and indices periodically.
- **Step eleven:** Analyse the productivity value and indices, seeking reasons why they increase or decrease and implement improvement action to correct problem areas and obtain a positive trend in productivity.
- **Step twelve:** Perform productivity evaluations periodically and focus on continuous assessment and improvement. Close open issues quickly and continually implement improvement action to correct poor performance.

Equal productivity curve

The equal productivity curve shown in Fig. 3.8 is a method of comparing the cost of two methods of production or service, each producing the same output. The equal productivity curve can also be constructed using total,

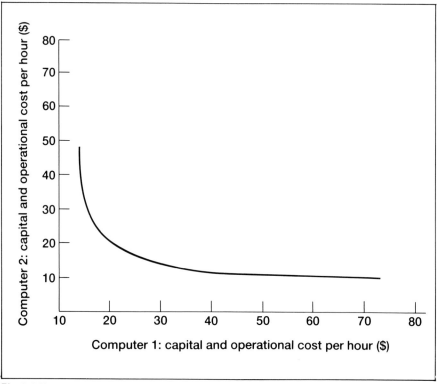

Fig. 3.8 Example of equal productivity curve.

total factor and partial productivities for two methods of production. It provides a quick assessment for choosing one of two methods. However, it should be used in conjunction with other productivity and quality tools for determining and selecting production tools and processes. The construction is essential based on the input and output monetary values of the production or service tools or process of interest.

Summary

The ability to use just-in-time production assessment and improvement tools in producing the input goods and services can make a difference in competitive world economy. In this section, several productivity assessment and improvement tools that can be used to structure production and service processes are offered. If applied correctly, these tools can yield significant benefits especially in eliminating waste, scrap, defects, bottlenecks, barriers, excessive inventory, process cycle time and chronic inspections. The use of the various techniques provided requires an integrated approach. A piecemeal approach should be discouraged. Teamwork is recommended for ensuring success.

Suggested reading

Ballakur, A. and Pratt, M. K. (1987), Integration of product and process design in high technology equipment production. Third IEEE International Electronics Manufacturing Technology Symposium Proceedings, Anaheim, October, pp. 220.

Crosby, L. B. (1984) The just-in-time manufacturing process: control of quality and quantity. *Production and Inventory Management*, Fourth Quarter, pp. 21–33.

Edosomwan, Johnson A. (1988). Improving productivity and quality at the source. Proceedings for the Annual International Industrial Engineering Conference, Orlando, Florida.

Edosomwan, Johnson A. (1988). *Integrating Productivity and Quality Management.* Marcel Dekker Inc., New York, New York.

Edosomwan, Johnson A. and Ballakur, Arvind (1988). *Improving Productivity and Quality in Electronics Assembly*, IIE Management Press and McGraw-Hill Book Company, New York.

Edosomwan, Johnson A. and Marsh, C. Streamlining materials flow for just-in-time production. Working Paper, *Industrial Engineering*.

Edwards, J. N. (1987). Integrating MRP-II with JIT: an update. APICS 30th Annual Conference Proceedings, p. 399.

Esrock, Y. D. (1985). The impact of reduced set-up time. *Production and Inventory Management*, Fourth Quarter, pp. 94–101.

Hall, R. W. (1983). *Zero Inventories.* Dow Jones-Irwin, Illinois.

Kim, T. M. (1985), Just-in-time manufacturing system: a periodic pull system. *International Journal of Production Research*, 23, pp. 553–562.

Leahy, J. A. (1984). Toyota production system – just in time, not just in Japan. *CIM Review*, Autumn, pp. 59.

Monden, Y. (1981). What makes the Toyota production system really tick? *Industrial Engineering*, January.

Monden, Y. (1981). Smoothed production lets Toyota adapt to demand changes and reduce inventory. *Industrial Engineering*, August.

Monden, Y. (1981). How Toyota shortened supply lot production time, waiting time and conveyance time. *Industrial Engineering*, September, pp. 22–30.

Monden, Y. (1983). Toyota production system. Industrial Engineering and Management Press, Norcross, Georgia.

Monden, Yasuhiro (1986). *Applying Just-in-Time: The American/Japanese Experience.* Industrial Engineering and Management Press, Norcross, Georgia.

Nakane, J. and Hall, R. W. (1983). Management specs for stockless production. *Harvard Business Review*, 61, pp. 84–91.

Nellemann, D. O. (1982). 'Just-in-Time' vs. just-in-case production/inventory systems; concepts borrowed back from Japan. *Production and Inventory Management*, 23, pp. 12–20.

Phadke, M. S. (1986). Design optimization case studies. *AT & T Technical Journal*, 65, p. 51.

Plenert, G. (1985). Are Japanese production methods applicable in the United States? *Production and Inventory Management*, 26, pp. 121–129.

Rice, J. W. (1982). A comparison of kanban and MRP concepts for the control of repetitive manufacturing systems. *Production and Inventory Management*, First Quarter, pp. 1–14.

Sandras, W. A., Jr (1987). Accelerated JIT/TQC implementation case studies. APICS 30th Annual Conference Proceedings.

Sandras, W. A., Jr (1984). Linking MRP and JIT: the best of the occident and the orient. Readings in zero inventory. APICS.

Sandras, W. A., Jr (1983). Continuous flow customized production. 1983 APICS Conference Proceedings.

Schonberger, R. J. (1986). The quality concept: still evolving. *National Productivity Review*, Winter.

Schonberger, R. J. (1983). Plant layout becomes product-oriented with cellular, just-in-time production concepts. *Industrial Engineering*, November.

Schonberger, R. J. (1983). Selecting the right manufacturing inventory system: western and Japanese approaches. *Production and Inventory Management*, Second Quarter.

Schonberger, R. J. (1987). *World Class Manufacturing Casebook – Implementing JIT and TQC*. The Free Press, New York.

Schoenberger, R. J. (1987). *Japanese Manufacturing Techniques – Nine Hidden Lessons in Simplicity*. The Free Press, New York.

Schorr, J. E. and Wallace, T. F. (1986). *High Performance Purchasing*. Oliver Wright Publications Limited.

Sepehri, M. (1985). How kanban system is used in American Toyota Motor Manufacturing. *Industrial Engineering*, pp. 50–56.

Sepehri, M. E. (1986). *Just-in-Time, Not Just-in-Japan – Case Studies of American Pioneers in JIT Implementation*. APICS, 500 West Annandale Road, Falls Church, VA.

Sepehri, M., Carlson, J. and Manrique, E. (1985). Material management at Toyota Japan and US. *1985 Annual IIE Conference Proceedings*, pp. 389–395.

Shingo, S. (1981). *Study of Toyota Production System*. Japan Management Association.

4

MANAGING THE CONNECTION AND RELATIONSHIPS BETWEEN PRODUCTIVITY AND QUALITY

Balancing total productivity and quality requirements

The ability to balance productivity and quality goals, objectives, resources and expected results, at the individual and organisational levels can make a difference in a competitive world economy. In this section, a specific framework, ideas and techniques are offered to assist industrial managers, decision-makers and workers to understand and properly manage the relationship and connection between productivity and quality.

Understanding the connection between productivity and quality

Productivity and quality are connected through:

● The organisation goal-setting process that determines the resources to be allocated to productivity and quality improvement projects.

- Measures of performance, effectiveness, efficiency and process value added by operational units.
- The relationship between the various inputs and outputs of a given production or service task.
- The techniques, tools and methods utilised to process the input resources.
- The process by which all resources are allocated to each task competing for use.
- The process boundaries relationships, connection and dependencies among supplier, process owner, customer and task execution stage.

Figure 4.1 presents the major components and elements that tie productivity and quality together. The need exists for ongoing effective management of the productivity and quality link in order to achieve expected output levels and desired quality levels. As we can observe in Fig. 4.1, any marginal change in one or more input will have impact on the total output and productivity levels. Also, marginal changes in the quality levels of any of the inputs will have impact on the overall quality and productivity levels. The mathematical relationships between productivity and quality are presented in the expressions and conditions presented below:

Let

$TPijt$ = Total productivity of task i, in site j, in period t.

$TOijt$ = Total output of task i, in site j, in period t. (Total output includes finished units, partial units and other output associated with input utilised.)

$QPijt$ = Quality of the product produced from task i, in site, j, in period t.

$TIijt$ = Total input utilised to produce output in task i, in site j, in period t. (Total output includes labour, materials, capital, energy, administrative expenses, computer operating expenses, robotics expenses, other technology input and miscellaneous expenses.)

$PRijt$ = Production rate of task i, in site j, in period t.

$WIijt$ = Work-in-process of task i, in site j, in period t.

$CRijt$ = Consumption rate of input of task i, in site j, in period t.

$SIijt$ = Supplier input of task i, in site j, in period t.

$TRijt$ = Total process requirement of task i, in site j, in period t.

$SSijt$ = Optimal steady state work-in-process level of task i, in site j, in period t.

$SLijt$ = Satisfaction level of customer using product of task i, in site j, in period t.

$DLijt$ = Marginal defect level that could occur in any of the inputs utilised to produce output in task i, in site j, in period t.

$TPijt$ = Marginal change in total productivity that could occur due to poor quality of any of the inputs utilised to produce output in task i, in site j, in period t.

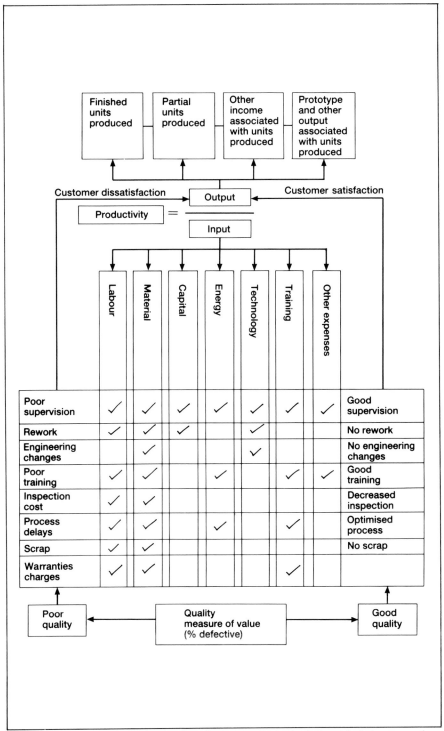

Fig. 4.1 A framework for understanding the connection and relationship between productivity and quality.

In general, productivity and quality improvement will occur if the following conditions are satisfied:

- **Condition one:** $PRijt = CRijt$
  Rate of production must be equal to the rate of consumption.
- **Condition two:** $WIijt \leqslant SSijt, WIijt = 0$ for ideal state.
  No inventory level is acceptable. Produce what is needed and not what is nice to have.
- **Condition three:** $SIijt = TRijt = CRijt$
  The rate at which the inputs are supplied must be equal to the rate at which they are utilised in the production process and must satisfy the consumption rate demanded by the customer.
- **Condition four:** $TOijt/TIijt = TPijt \geqslant 1$
  The total productivity of a given task at a specific time period must be positive to reflect effective utilisation of resources. The relationship between inputs and outputs must be managed closely to ensure that total productivity is maximised.
- **Condition five:** $\triangle DLijt = 0$ at $t = 1,2,3...,n$
  No level of defect is acceptable for all output produced.
- **Condition six:** $TPijt = 0$ at $t = 1,2,3,...,n$
  No negative change in productivity level due to poor quality of any input is acceptable.
- **Condition seven:** $SLijt \geqslant 100\%; QPijt = E+$
  The satisfaction level of every customer receiving the final product or service must meet expectation through the quality of products and services offered.
- **Condition eight:** $TOijt \uparrow \quad TIijt \downarrow$
  Productivity increases due to the utilisation of minimum input to produce more output.
- **Condition nine:** $TOijt \uparrow \quad \overline{TIijt}$
  Productivity increases due to the fact that more output is obtained by keeping the level of input utilised constant.
- **Condition ten:** $TOijt \uparrow \quad RH, TIijt \uparrow \quad RL$
  Productivity increases due to higher rate of increase in output compared to lower rate of increase in input.
- **Condition eleven:** $\overline{TOijt}, TIijt \downarrow$
  Productivity increases due to decreases in the amount of input required to produce required output.
- **Condition twelve:** $TOijt, \downarrow \quad TIijt \downarrow \quad RL$
  Productivity increases due to less consumption of input, although output decreases marginally.
- **Condition thirteen:** $\sum \triangle DLijt = 0$ at $t = 1,2,3,...,n$
  The marginal direct levels from all the inputs must be zero at all times. No defective parts or other inputs should be used in the production and service process.

- **Condition fourteen:** *SLijt* ↑ *TPijt* ↑ , *QPijt* ↑
  Increases in productivity and improvement in quality leads to more customer satisfaction.

Where i = 1,2,3,...,k, t = 1,2,3,...,n, j = 1,2,3,...,m E+ = quality excellence, ↑ = rate of increase, ↓ = rate of decrease, - = constant rate, ↓ RL = decreases at lower rate, ↑ RH = increases at higher rate, ↑ RL = increases at lower rate.

Productivity and quality lever of balance

Figure 4.2 presents the lever involved in balancing productivity and quality in the business process. The total productivity and quality level of balance shows the various variables that must be managed continuously to provide excellence in productivity and quality. The notion that increases in productivity and improved quality are impossible should be disregarded. Increased productivity and improved quality is quite possible if one is committed and willing to balance the apparent contradictory sets of goals and objectives.

Productivity and quality requirements should be managed together. The people and various functions that work to produce the final output for the organisation must be willing to coexist and work together. Effective teamwork can go a long way to insure that both the production manager and the quality manager meet the end objective – providing quality product to the customer.

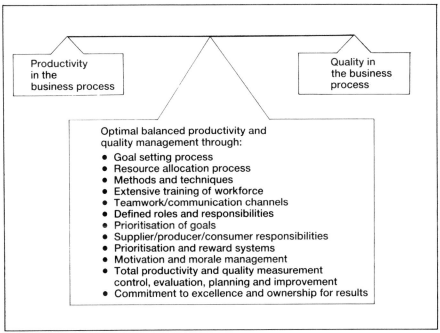

Fig. 4.2 Productivity and quality lever of balance.

One approach for balancing productivity and quality results at the individual level is to use the productivity and quality task responsibility curve (PQTRC), presented in Fig. 4.3, to assess individual workload. At point *A* on the PQTRC an individual experiences low productivity and quality due to underload or boredom. The strategy is to employ specific improvement techniques to move individual performance from point *A* to *B*. Through the application of appropriate workload balancing technique the individuals performance at point *C* can also be brought to the optimum balance point *B*. Maintaining performance level in point *B* always requires:

- Proper training and education.
- Providing the right tools.
- Setting the right priorities.
- Allocating resources efficiently.
- Continually balancing workload
- Appropriate direction on what is to be accomplished.

The learning curve concept can also be applied when stabilising individual performance using PQTRC. The typical effect of the learning curve shown in Fig. 4.4 can be to pin-point the degree at which human performance improves due to reinforcement and frequent task repetitions. As shown n Fig. 4.4, productivity benefit due to learning is realised usually in the early stages of the production or service run. The idea is to recognise the point at which the learning curve begins to flatten due to process changes,

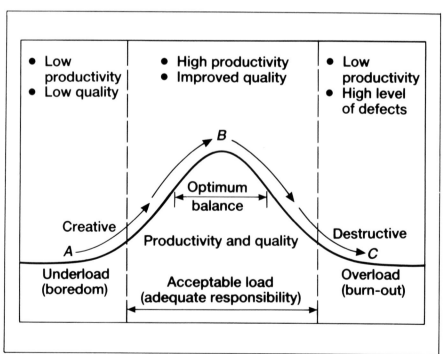

Fig 4.3 Productivity and quality task responsibility curve.

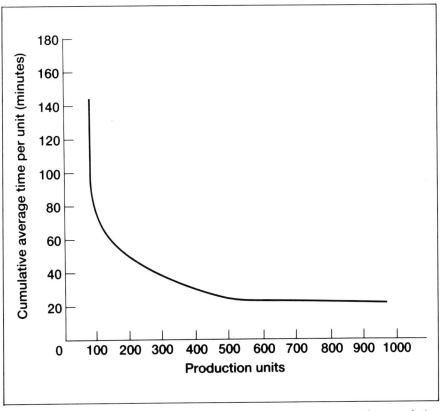

Fig. 4.4 Example of cumulative production (part units) learning curve for cumulative production.

or other intervening variables. In general, a learning curve can be represented on log paper as follows:

$$\log CA_x = \log CF_1 + n\log X$$

where CA_x = cumulative total average cost of x units, CF_1 = cost of the first unit, X = total number cumulative units to be produced and n = slope of learning curve.

The slope of the learning curve can be obtained as follows:

$$n = \frac{\log CF_1 - \log CF_2}{\log P_1 - \log P_2}$$

Where
    CF_1 = average cumulative cost per unit at the first production level, CF_2 = average cumulative cost per unit at the second production level, P_1 = production volume at the first production level and P_2 production volume at the second production level.

The balancing of productivity and quality goals, resource allocation, and expected output should be done at the individual, task, department, and organisation level. The degree of success depends on how well employees and management choose to operate a formal productivity and quality programme. Management must be willing to commit investment and resources to productivity and quality programmes that have both short-term and long-term payoff. Perhaps the proper measure of a balanced productivity and quality programme is the degree in which everyone in the organisation is willing to take ownership for and pride in the final work output that goes to the customer.

Productivity and quality management model (PQMM)

The components of the productivity and quality management model (PQMM) are presented in Fig. 4.5 A and B. The PQMM is provided to aid both management and employees in managing productivity and quality at the source. The implementation of PQMM through a formal productivity and quality management programme is highly recommended. Such a programme should have in place the following:

- Work processes that are classified by product mix, procedures, people, systems requirement, and man–machine interaction.
- Personnel training that provides the basis for the effective and efficient use of resources.
- A system for managing the input and output components of work cells, work flow pattern and the interdependencies among production and service variables.
- A productivity and quality measurement, control, evaluation, planning and improvement techniques and methods.
- A system for ongoing problem root cause analysis, and implementation of improvement actions.

   Using CPQMM of balance productivity and quality results, also requires that the following conditions be satisfied:

- **Condition one:** The rate of production must be equal to the rate of consumption. Produce only what is needed and not what is nice to have.
- **Condition two:** Production and service errors that affect productivity and quality are to be controlled.
- **Condition three:** There is total impact assessment for all changes made to service and production processes, policies and procedures.
- **Condition four:** No output goes out of the production and service loop to the customer unless it is perfect.
- **Condition five:** Increasing the layers of management, processes, and procedures to cause bottle-necks is to be discouraged.

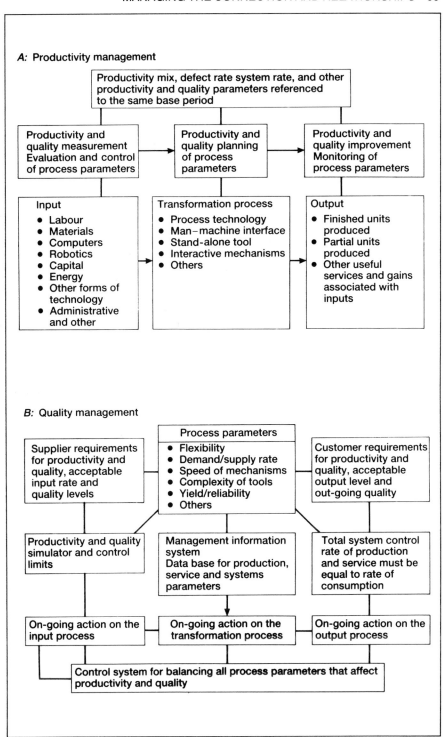

Fig. 4.5 Components of the PQMM. A productivity components; B quality management components.

Productivity and quality assessment matrix (PAQAM)

The PAQAM, shown in Fig.4.6, is provided as an aid to industrial managers, decision makers, and workers interested in balancing productivity and quality expected results. PAQAM can be used to assess the productivity and quality position periodically at the individual, task, department, and firm levels. A five-step approach presented below should be followed when using PAQAM in the work environment:

- **Step one:** Train everyone on productivity and quality management concepts and techniques. Understand the input and output elements of each task or organisation unit, the workflow pattern, procedures, and personnel.

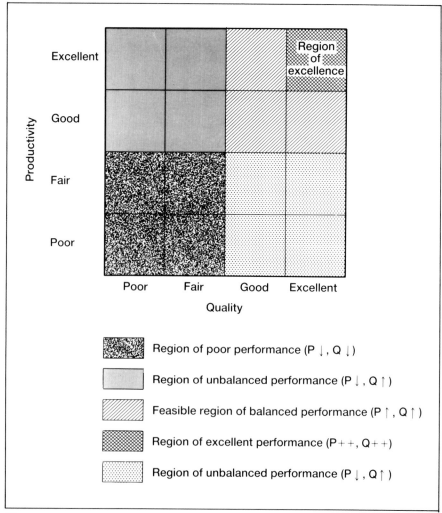

Fig 4.6 Productivity and quality assessment matrix (PAQAM).

- **Step two:** Develop and implement measurement methods for productivity and quality at the individual, task and organisational levels. Partial factor, total factor and total productivity values and indices are recommended. Per cent defective, quality index, internal failure costs, external failure costs, appraisal costs, and prevention costs are recommended as adequate measures of quality.
- **Step three:** Classify the productivity and quality measures obtained in Step two in four major categories: poor, fair, good, and excellent. Plot the values obtained in the PAQAM assessment matrix.
- **Step four:** Perform a root cause analysis to determine why a particular performance appears on each region. Implement improvement actions to correct and move a poorly performing individual or task to the region of productivity and quality excellence.
- **Step five:** Follow up periodically on open issues. Train everyone in the organisation to use PAQAM to assess his own productivity and quality position. Base productivity and quality rewards on balanced accomplishments.

Correcting poor performance

- Provide on-going counselling and feedback on performance level. Let a poorly performing individual know how well he or she is doing on the job.
- Provide the required class-room training to correct deficiency in skill level.
- Provide the required on-the-job training (coaching) to correct deficiency in skill level.
- Match skills to the right job. Try job rotation.
- Use experienced personnel who perform highly to train poorly performing individuals.
- Let the poorly performing individual accept ownership on gradual improvement steps to correct low performance level.
- Reward improvement promptly by appropriate feedback.

Cost of quality and productivity improvement

Ideally one would like to obtain excellent product and service quality, and productivity improvement, at no cost. It costs money to build quality into production and service processes; and to obtain productivity improvement at the source of production and service. My own experience, combined with data from many manufacturing and service industries shows the distribution of quality costs to be as presented in Fig. 4.7. Quality costs and productivity improvement costs can be defined as follows.

Prevention costs

Prevention costs are costs associated with designing, implementing and maintaining a quality system capable of anticipating and preventing quality problems before they generate avoidable costs. All costs related to efforts in design and manufacturing that are directed toward the prevention of non-conformance are in this category. Such costs, typically, include the costs of training, new products review, burn-in, problem solving and consulting, quality planning, quality control system, and user, supplier and customer testing of quality control system.

Appraisal costs

Appraisal costs are costs incurred to detect errors. These costs are associated with measuring, evaluating, or auditing products, processes, components, and purchased materials to assure conformance to quality standards and performance specifications. Such costs include the costs of inspection and testing of incoming parts or materials, equipment maintenance for accuracy and reliability, costs of verification of process performance and materials and services consumed in destructive test cycles.

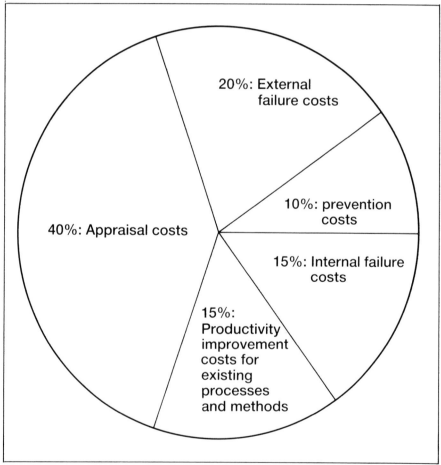

Fig. 4.7 Estimated per cent of total cost of quality and productivity improvement in manufacturing and service organisations.

Internal failure costs

Internal failure costs are associated with defective products, components, and materials that fail to meet quality requirements, where this failure is discovered prior to delivery of the product to the customer. Internal failure costs can also be defined as costs incurred in correcting the errors at the appraisal process before delivery of the product to the ultimate customer. Such costs typically include costs of failure analysis, rework and repairs, cost of wasted tools and equipment, yield losses, re-testing of products after rework, off-specing, and scrap control.

External failure costs

External failure costs are costs incurred in correcting errors after delivery of the product to the customer. These costs are generated by defective products or services offered to the customer. The products or services, generally, fail to satisfy the customer requirements and do not conform to requirements. Such costs include warranty charges, liability costs, penalties, interest payment due to late deliveries of products and services, error investigation charges, transportation to and from customer site, and indirect costs.

Productivity improvement costs

Productivity improvement costs are costs incurred for evaluating existing production and service processes for improvement, and designing and implementing new ideas and methods to correct problems at the source of production and service. Such costs include current process layout evaluation, process redesign, elimination of process bottle-necks, direct and indirect costs of implementing new improvement projects and improvement tools.

Minimising the cost of quality and productivity improvement. The following steps are recommended for reducing and minimising the cost of quality and productivity improvement:

- **Step one:** Start with a specific operation unit or task and identify a specific quality problem or productivity improvement need.
- **Step two:** Understand each element involved in each operation unit and develop the distribution of quality costs, process bottle-necks and barriers.
- **Step three:** Identify the input and output of the operation unit including the transformation process. Emphasis should be placed on the following: labour, materials, capital, energy, administrative inputs, finished units, partial units, work-in-process, data on employee performance, department activity lists, customer, supplier and process owners activity lists.
- **Step four:** Identify the effort spent on all activities, tasks, and improvement projects, and develop the cost of quality and productivity

improvement. A typical monthly st of quality and productivity improvement for a medium-sized shoe manufacturer is presented in Fig. 4.8.

- **Step five:** Determine the sources of errors and error types and pin-point specific reasons for errors by tasks and for each operational unit.
- **Step six:** Develop solutions to eliminate errors, process bottle-necks and barriers. The solutions should address both internal and external generated errors.
- **Step seven:** Implement suggested solutions, monitor results and periodically perform activities in all the steps above.

Summary

This section has presented practical tools and a framework for balancing productivity and quality requirements, and for managing the relationship between productivity and quality at the source of production and service. Implementation of the productivity and quality lever of balance requires management and employees to attend to productivity and quality improvement issues at the strategic, tactical and operational planning stages in

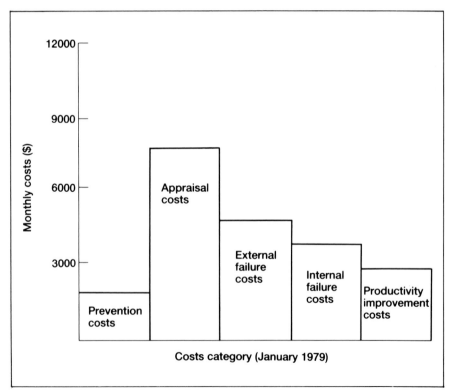

Fig. 4.8 Cost of quality and productivity improvement for a shoe manufacturer (January 1979).

organisations. The productivity and quality management tools present essential components that must be managed continuously in both the production and service environments. Through continuous improvement efforts, improvements in quality and productivity can be achieved. The productivity and quality assessment matrix presented should be used as a tool for improving poor performance in productivity and quality and not as a penalty tool for individuals or operation units. The assessment of cost of quality and productivity improvement is provided, with a step-by-step approach for reducing such costs.

Suggested reading

Deming, W. Edwards (1981). Improvement of quality and productivity through action by management. *National Productivity Review*, 1, pp.12–22.

Edosomwan, Johnson A. (1986). Productivity and quality management – a challenge in the year 2000. Proceedings of Annual International Industrial Engineering Conference, Boston, Massachusetts.

Edosomwan, Johnson A. (1987). *Integrating Productivity and Quality Management*. Marcel Dekker Inc., New York.

Edosomwan, Johnson A. (1988). Improving productivity and quality at the source. Proceedings for the Annual International Industrial Engineering Conference, Orlando, Florida.

Edosomwan, Johnson A. (1989). A framework for balancing productivity and quality requirements in organisations. Working Paper for the Second International Conference on Productivity Research, Miami Florida.

Feigenbaum, Armand (1984). The hard road to quality excellence. *National Productivity Review*, 3, pp.442–445.

Sephehri, Mehran (1987). *Quest for Quality: Managing the Total System*. Industrial Engineering and Management Press, Atlanta, Georgia.

5 IMPLEMENTING AND MAINTAINING PRODUCTIVITY AND QUALITY IMPROVEMENT PROJECTS

Recommended process improvement methodology

The following steps are recommended for improving production and service processes:

- **Step one:** Understand the current process and the task boundaries (process, customer, cross functional and supplier). Perform a thorough analysis of all production and service variables (people, equipment, materials, etc).
- **Step two:** Create a realistic awareness or a vision of the improved process. Convince others that a breakthrough is needed, convince the team involved that improvement in productivity and quality is possible and desirable.

- **Step three:** Specify opportunity for improvement by key process parameters and areas. Identify the important projects. Focus on the productivity and quality problems that are most important.
- **Step four:** Specify the scope of the improvement effort by process at the task level. Define responsibility and ownership for results.
- **Step five:** Organise for breakthrough in knowledge and specify the mechanisms for obtaining required knowledge. Advice from experienced experts in productivity and quality improvement can lead to sources for obtaining the missing knowledge.
- **Step six:** Pilot the proposed improvement in the process. Focus on the most important vital few projects
- **Step seven:** Conduct productivity and quality improvement analysis. Collect and analyse data and facts that are required and recommend the specific process improvement action needed.
- **Step eight:** Implement the recommended improvement techniques, tools and methods. Institutionalise the new ideas in the process.
- **Step nine:** Evaluate and verify that proposed improvement occurred. Obtain feedback from both management and employees on the proposed improvement.
- **Step ten:** Ensure that action plans are in place to control resource utilisation.
- **Step eleven:** Monitor results from the new mix of resources to ensure that expected outcomes are obtained. Determine the effect of proposed changes on people, process and organisation involved and develop strategies to overcome the resistance to change.
- **Step twelve:** Follow-up periodically and repeat all steps for new opportunities. Implement adequate controls to hold the new level of improvement in productivity and quality.

The 6C principles for implementing productivity and quality improvement projects

In order to assist industrial managers, productivity and quality improvement analysts to be successful in managing productivity and quality improvement projects, the comprehensive use of the 6C principles shown in Fig. 5.1 of control, co-ordination, co-operation, contribution analysis, communication and cost avoidance is recommended:

Principle one. Controls – provide controls to monitor productivity and quality improvement projects

In managing productivity and quality issues and projects, it is important to define the objectives and understand the activities involved. Specific performance parameters such as productivity ratios, cost curves and control

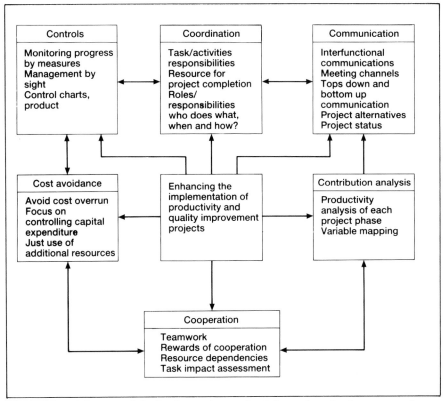

Fig. 5.1 The 6C framework for implementing productivity and quality improvement projects.

charts should be used in measuring the results of implementing the objectives. In addition, the schedule for the various activities have to be identified. Two techniques are recommended for controlling all the elements involved in a specific project:

- Gantt chart: A Gantt chart, shown in Fig. 5.2, provides a means for arranging the list of activities to be accomplished, arranged vertically, with the time of completion stated horizontally. The analyst monitors the completion of each task and tracks unfinished tasks periodically until completed.
- Pert chart: The Pert, chart shown in Fig. 5.3, provides a means for managing the probability of success for each task and highlights the earliest and latest times a given task can be accomplished.

Principle two. Coordination – provide a focal point for the coordination of productivity and quality improvement projects.

The implementation of a new idea that improves productivity and quality in the workplace requires a focal point for the coordination of all activities. This can be achieved by designating a project manager to be in charge of all

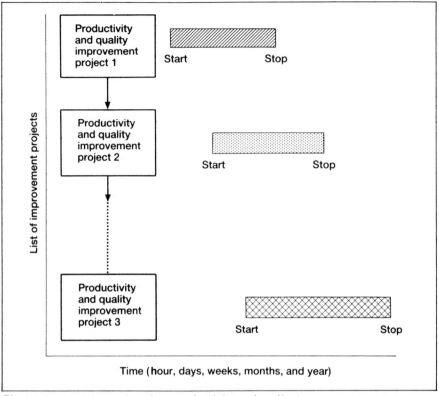

Fig. 5.2 A typical Gantt chart for a productivity and quality improvement project.

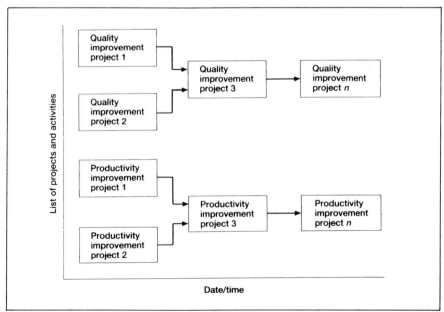

Fig. 5.3 A typical Pert chart for managing productivity and quality improvement projects.

activities. The project manager, working with other members of the project team, ensures that all project resources are controlled and allocated properly, and ensures that the project is going according to schedule. The project manager requires a good database and tracking mechanisms for all activities. The successful project manager is one who has good interpersonal skills, good organisation and planning abilities and good judgement.

Principle three. Communication – provide adequate communication channels

The status of a productivity and quality improvement project must be reviewed periodically by the people involved. Usually, the project manager ensures that regular meetings are held to discuss open issues that require resolution and also to obtain status on key accomplishments. On-going communication among project team members is required to avoid things falling through the cracks. Involve team members, vendors, and management in all project review process.

Principle four. Cost avoidance – provide adequate focus on cost avoidance

In order to avoid cost overrun in productivity and quality improvement projects implementations, the project implementation phases cost posture should be monitored. Additional features or functions without value added should be avoided. Careful attention must be paid to capital expenditure on fixtures, programming, manpower, and contractors at each phase of the project implement. In situations where vendors are responsible for project implementation, periodic cost postures must be requested and reviewed by the project leader.

Principle five. Contribution of analysis – implement measures to monitor the contribution of each phase of productivity and quality improvement projects.

Each implementation phase of a technology project should provide tangible results. For example, the machine characterisation phase should enable the project leader to understand the pattern of performance for a given machine. The contribution analysis of each phase of the improvement project can be performed by using the variable and result mapping technique. This technique requires that for each activity or task performed the expected result must be matched against the true output or result. This provides a quick way of identifying deviations from project goals and objectives as well as of understanding the causes of deviation from specifications. The variable mapping technique requires that action be put in place to resolve project deviations promptly.

Principle six. Co-operation – facilitate co-operation among project participants.

The co-operation between members of the project implementation team is a key requirement for success. If possible, the teamwork process should involve the designer, developer, implementers, and users of the new method or ideas. Where the physical presence of all the functional areas is impossible, communication channels should be put in place to facilitate information-sharing to promote co-operation. The understanding of the goals and objectives behind the implementation of a new technology in the workplace by all members of the organisation facilitates co-operation. Such understanding can be accomplished through project kick-off meetings at various levels of the organisation.

Monitoring progress and process improvement ownership management

The monitoring of productivity and quality improvement projects is a very essential step in ensuring that suggested creative ideas and methods are implemented to improve productivity and quality at the source. The following ideas are recommended for monitoring process improvement projects.

- Document the savings related to specific improvement projects by using one of the following criteria: defect levels, job satisfaction and improvement in morale, conformation of specific improvement to policy and standard time, total productivity measures, cost-benefit analysis and financial ratios.
- Define the scope of each specific productivity and quality improvement project with specific focus on:

  - Who should do what?
  - What is the purpose of the improvement project?
  - Where is the improvement to be implemented?
  - When should the improvement project be completed?
  - How should the improvement project be done?

  The key elements of the process improvement ownership management is specified in Fig 5.4. Each of the elements specified must be managed continuously in order to obtain anticipated productivity and quality results.

- Hold productivity and quality improvement meetings periodically to track results and the status of improvement projects. In order for such meetings to be effective they must be conducted using the following guidelines:

  - Define the meeting times, objectives, agenda and location ahead of time and let everyone involved in the improvement project have the meeting notice ahead of time.
  - Identify the chairperson for the meeting. This person should be familiar with the productivity and quality improvement project. Usually the chairperson specifies the objectives for the meeting.

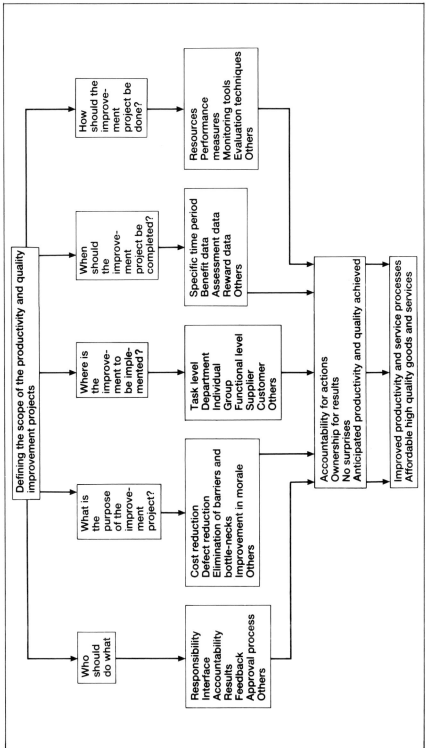

Fig. 5.4 Elements of process improvement ownership management.

- Specify attendee roles and provide specific time slots for each attendee to present his role. Allow time for group discussions on specific issues presented.
- Follow the agenda provided and monitor time and topic closely.
- Ensure that everyone present at the meeting concentrates on the specific productivity and quality improvement topic.
- Record the issues, discussions and matters presented during the meeting. Summarise the results of the meeting and ensure that everyone is aware of the subject covered.
- Stop the meeting on time and establish a follow-up agenda if required.

Strategies for overcoming common implementation problems

Whenever a new programme, or process improvement idea is promoted for implementation there are bound to be problems. Edosomwan (1987a, pp 266–269) identified the most frequent types of implementation problems and solution strategies and these are discussed below.

Unwillingness to change work habit

After learning a given pattern to perform a specific task, the pattern becomes a habit. It is often difficult to break away from the old habit and accept a new one. People must be educated about what the new productivity and quality improvement will bring to their tasks, and, in addition, must be made to understand both the tangible and intangible benefits of changing from an old habit to a new one. A good strategy is to get everyone involved in all phases of the projects and programmes when possible.

Resistance to change

Whenever a new programme or idea is promoted, people will accept or resist change depending on how they are affected by the change. There are four types of people one is likely to deal with when promoting productivity and quality improvements. There are those who will do everything within their power to defeat the improvement scheme because it creates an extra burden for them. Such people always find several reasons why the new improvement idea will not work. They always try to convince the improvement analyser to stay with the old method of doing things. There are those who do all the talking about how productivity and quality should be improved and promoted but take very little action. There are others who also spend their energy wishing someone else or some new system will automatically do the work. And, finally, there are those people with a keen interest in improving productivity and quality so that the organisation can stay profitable. Such people get under the load, do the work, and provide all the support needed. The strategy is to be able to get all the four categories of people convinced to a great extent. This can be done through emphasis on teamwork and regular meetings to ensure effective communication of the selected improvement programmes. It is also recommended that the co-operative efforts received be recognised among peers and supervisors.

Lack of proper planning

A productivity and quality improvement programme can easily be un-successful if the requirements for start-up, key people, and total implemen-tation of activities are not planned properly. It is important for the appropriate trained people with knowledge of productivity and quality to be made coordinators of improvement projects. Such coordinators must specify in great detail the key activities needed for improvement projects, who is responsible, when they will be completed, and the expected benefit date.

Fear of the unknown

New productivity and quality improvement ideas may have some uncer-tainty, because of unproven results, and most people are likely to be afraid of failure. As a result, they may resist the implementation of new concepts and ideas. All levels of management and employees must be educated about the essentials and the importance of willingness to risk failure. If one new idea fails, it does not prevent another good one from succeeding.

Lack of appropriate database

A productivity and quality improvement programme should be based on an adequate database with correct historical information. It is very impor-tant to involve all levels of management and employees during improve-ment programme start-ups to ensure that adequate data and a description of processes and procedures are provided.

Resentment of criticism

Most people believe that they perform their task in the most effective and efficient manner and will resent criticism that proves otherwise. Criticism from productivity analysts, coordinators, and consultants should be offered constructively and positively to avoid backlash. On the other hand, those receiving ideas must be willing to do away with a defensive attitude. Eve-ryone involved in the productivity and quality improvement programme must have an open mind and the willingness to accommodate several diffe-rent viewpoints.

Inadequate sharing of productivity and quality improvement gains

Productivity and quality gains obtained from improvement programmes must be distributed equitably and fairly to encourage a continued innovative process for additional ideas. Most organisations have formal suggestion programmes, cost effectiveness programmes, bonus programmes, and awards programmes that are specifically designed to reward contributions to productivity and quality improvement. It is important to recognise that money is not the only source of motivation. Peer and superior recognition, promotions, additional challenges, job content, and others are also key sources of motivation.

Conflicting compromise of objectives

Productivity and quality improvement go together. Both managers and employees must stay away from the notion that if productivity improves, quality will suffer. The typical notion of push schedules when they are needed and push quality when it is wanted should basically be eliminated. Programmes selected for improvements must satisfy dual objectives. People must be trained in how to manage conflicting objectives.

Complacency resulting from current status

There is a tendency for those organisations that are already leaders in their respective industrial sector to feel so satisfied with their performance as leaders that they completely ignore the ongoing assessment of the method of operation and recommendations for implementable changes. Everyone within the organisation must be trained to recognise that there is no limit to success through improvement. The more improvement ideas are implemented, the better off the organisation will be financially.

Starting off too big

Productivity and quality improvement issues can get complicated. The entire organisation's problem cannot be resolved overnight. For improvement programmes to be successful, they must be started with reasonable projects that the available resources can handle. Once the results and benefits of such projects have been obtained, bigger ventures can be considered.

Handling cultural resistance and organisational barriers

I found the following recommendations offered by Juran and Gryna (1980, pp. 127–128) to be useful in managing productivity and quality improvement projects:

- Establish the need for the change in terms that are important to the people involved rather than on the basis of the logic of the change.
- Use participation to get ideas on both the technical and social aspects of the change.

  - Know the people for whom the change is intended. What are their short and long-range goals, their problems, etc.?
  - Announce the need for a change and provide for participation of those concerned as early as possible.
  - Use the members of the culture (maybe the steering arm) to furnish advice on the possible social effects of a technological change.
  - Where a change is to be made in the work system for a group of workers, allow the workers to create as much of the change as possible.
  - Consider using a 'change catalyst' to help in the planning and implementation of the change. The change catalyst is a respected person who can supply objectivity to the analysis and implementation.
  - Answer suggestions from workers promptly and in a manner that shows respect for the worker.
  - Treat all people with dignity.
  - Keep the change relatively small so that it can be introduced gradually and modified as experience dictates. Build major programmes on a foundation of previous successes.
  - Produce rewarding results early.
  - Guard against surprises by keeping everyone informed.

- Gain agreement on the change.

  - Try persuasion to secure change. Much depends here on the extent of prior participation and on the extent to which the individual is 'treated with dignity'.
  - Change the environment in a way that makes it easy for the individual to change his point of view.
  - Remedy the causes of resistance from any of the line personnel.
  - Create a social climate that favours the new habits.
  - Explain what each person must do under the new procedure. What must they do 'different'?
  - Eliminate technical jargon in explaining the change.
  - Reduce the impact of changes by weaving them into an existing broader pattern of behaviour, or by letting them ride in on the back of some acceptable change.
  - Put yourself in the other person's place.

Overcoming common problems and avoiding failure

The implementation of a new productivity and quality improvement idea in the workplace is perhaps one of the most difficult tasks to accomplish.

Most of the difficulty is centred on human resistance to change and unwillingness to accept new change and work methods. Most productivity and quality improvement ideas fail, not because they are not good, but because the ingredients and mechanisms for implementation were not carried out properly. The following guidelines are recommended when implementing new productivity and quality improvement projects, programmes, methods and ideas:

- Understand the organisation climate and culture and obtain the total support of everyone, including suppliers and vendors.
- Outline specific implementation steps for each improvement project including detailed activity lists, target and benefit dates of completion.
- Ensure that the productivity and quality improvement goals and objectives are realistic and open to opportunity.
- Ensure that improvement goals and objectives maximise the effective use of available resources.
- Plan implementation activities ahead of time, taking into account the deliverables from supplier, vendors, task and process owners.
- Maintain internal and external contacts with key people who have the expertise to help and train workforce members in new techniques for productivity and quality improvement. Do not re-invent the wheel.
- Establish a clear review process for concerns and accomplishments that may arise.
- Re-evaluate the programme periodically, and make modifications when necessary.
- Be flexible and willing to sacrifice time and other resources to obtain improvement.
- Follow-up continuously to resolve open issues.
- Do not expect too great a productivity and quality improvement overnight.
- Use expert opinions and take advice when needed.
- Obtain adequate staffing to complete the improvement programme objectives.
- Do not expect too great an immediate return on investment. Some improvement projects may have key benefits because they provide continuous growth in the long run.
- Sell the benefits of the new idea effectively to the total organisation and show implementation progress to everyone involved.
- Motivate people to do their best and reward accomplishments promptly.
- Resolve open issues quickly and advise all parties concerned.
- Find out who has implemented such productivity and quality ideas before, and learn from their experience.
- Encourage a positive team attitude and strong enthusiasm to succeed on new ventures. Use participative management style to build a climate that fosters cooperation and total involvement of both management and employees.

● Document results before and after implementation of the new productivity and quality idea. Focus on selling the benefits of the new method and idea.

Essential elements for encouraging teamwork

Although high-level, individual performance and creativity improves productivity and quality, teamwork from the total organisation, departments and functional areas is essential for continued improvement in productivity and quality at the source of production or service. As shown in Fig. 5.5, the productivity and quality improvement process requires total team involvement. The win-win attitude from everyone is essential in achieving success while managing the complex relationships between input-process-output of production and service systems. The following elements can foster good teamwork.

Fig. 5.5 Total team involvement in productivity and quality improvement process.

- Good management that maintains a balance between people and product management, as well as encouraging a participative approach to business management. Such participative style allows for input to decision making, provides worker control over jobs, encourages innovation, ownership for results and accountability for actions.
- Appropriate defined mission for individuals and the organisation. The goals of the organisation and of individuals must complement each other. Everyone within the organisation must be aware of the common goals and their role and required contributions to meet the end objectives.
- An environment that allows people to strive toward common objectives and results. Break down the barriers between management, functional areas and departments. Recognise both individual and group performance.
- Adequate communication channels and information that enhances group knowledge and builds trust among people.
- The right vision that seeks teamwork as a source of strength and not a threat.
- Adequate focus and balance between the desires and needs of individuals, the team and the organisation goal and objectives. Encourage teamwork along the line of a common goal which requires interdependence.

Management attention is required on an on-going basis to the people management issues that affect teamwork, cause friction and affect productivity and quality improvement. The right management attention should provide an open door policy that allows individuals and teams to discuss people and product management problems honestly in a non-threatening manner, with the focus on respect for the individual opinions, ideas and values while achieving positive results from everyone.

Summary

The implementation of a new productivity and quality idea in the workplace is perhaps one of the most challenging experiences for decision makers and improvement analysts. Through the teamwork approach and the comprehensive implementation of the 6C principles of control, co-ordination, co-operation, contribution analysis, communication and cost avoidance, productivity and quality ideas can be implemented without tears and pain. It is recommended that both management and employees take a leadership role in promoting productivity and quality improvement with strong enthusiasm and confidence. Everyone within the organisation must be committed and concerned that there is a better way of improving the various tasks and activities performed.

Suggested reading

Deming, W. Edwards (1982). *Quality, Productivity and Competitive Position.* MIT Press.

Edosomwan, Johnson A. (1987a). *Integrating Productivity and Quality Management,* Marcel Dekker Inc., New York.

Edosomwan, Johnson A. (1987b). A program for managing productivity and quality. *Industrial Engineering Journal,* January.

Edosomwan, Johnson A. (1987c). The challenge for industrial managers: productivity and quality in the workplace. *Industrial Management,* September/October.

Juran, J. M. and Gryna, F. M. Jr (1980). *Quality Planning and Analysis.* McGraw-Hill Book Company, New York.

APPENDIX A: PRODUCTIVITY AND QUALITY MANAGEMENT EXERCISES

Question 1 a Refer to Fig. A.1. Define a new process and present the rationale that supports your process design for the PCB process.
b What steps should be taken to build quality into your suggested PCB process?
c How should productivity and quality requirements be managed?
d How would you proceed to implement a statistical process control programme?

Question 2 A tough production manager wishes to reduce defect level of TV units by 15%, improve productivity by 35%, reduce work-in-process inventory by 10%, reduce manpower by 18% and increase employee salaries by 20% per year. How can Mr. Tough Manager achieve these apparently contradictory objectives?

Question 3 How would you go about implementing techniques to improve productivity and quality at the source? Identify dependencies, and present your ideas in a logical flow.

Question 4 Demonstrate through practical examples how and why productivity and quality are related and connected. How should industrial managers balance quality and productivity improvement goals in the business process?

Question 5 Discuss and present an example to illustrate how a specific productivity improvement programme can fail.

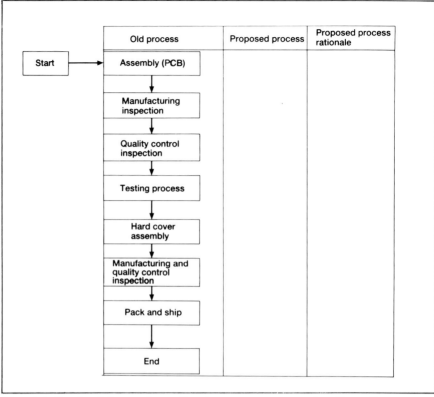

Fig. A.1 Productivity and quality improvement exercise flow diagram.

Question 6 Is there any relationship between productivity measurement and planning? How should productivity planning be implemented in organisations?

Question 7 "If you cannot measure the performance of a process you cannot control and improve it." Do you agree with the above statement? Why or why not?

Question 8 Discuss the Edosomwan twelve principles for productivity and quality management. How would you go about implementing the ten principles in a manufacturing or service work environment?

Question 9 Discuss how the motivation and morale level of employees can affect total productivity. Is the strategy that achieves profit by laying off workers adequate? Why or why not? How should industrial managers deal with tough economic times?

Question 10 The data presented in Table A.1 were collected for the Johnson computer company PCB process. Each sample checks 200 PCBs. Calculate the control units for the following:
  (1) *NP* Chart
  (2) *P* Chart
  (3) *C* Chart
  (4) *U* Chart

Table A.1 PCB process data

Sample (n)	Defective (np)	Fraction defective (p)	Defects (c)	Defects per unit (u)
1	13	.065	20	.10
2	8	.04	11	.055
3	10	.05	13	.065
4	15	.075	25	.123
5	12	.06	18	.09
6	9	.045	13	.065
7	6	.03	10	.05
8	4	.02	8	.04
9	7	.035	11	.055
10	11	.055	16	.08
11	14	.07	20	.10
12	10	.05	17	.085
13	7	.035	10	.05
14	9	.045	12	.06
15	12	.06	15	.075
16	13	.065	19	.095
17	8	.04	14	.07
18	11	.055	16	.08
19	9	.045	13	.065
20	12	.06	13	.09
21	15	.075	21	.105
22	11	.055	19	.095
23	8	.04	11	.055
24	6	.03	8	.04
25	10	.05	12	.06
Total	250		370	

a Indicate how the various charts and control limits should be used to improve quality in the business process.

b How would you go about implementing a computer-assisted data collection system for the PCB process?

c How would you go about selling the benefits of statistical process control to the management of the Johnson Computer Company?

Question 11 The data presented in Table A.2 represent input and output elements data from a robotic-aided assembly task for Motor West Company. The deflators were provided from the consumer price indexes published by the Bureau of Labor Statistics.

a Calculate the total and partial productivity values and indices.

b Explain how you can apply the productivity values and indices as a basis for productivity planning and improvement.

Question 12 Are incentive and suggestion programmes the answer to productivity improvement? Why or why not? What are the benefits and disadvantages of quality circle programmes?

Question 13 Explain the meaning of just-in-time productivity and quality improvement. Present a step-by-step approach for designing and implementing JIT in a typical hamburger restaurant.

Table A.2 *Productivity measurement data for motor invest company*

Item	Period		
	March 1988	*April 1988*	*May 1988*
Output			
a Finished units	$5500	$8800	$4891
b Partial units	$1850	$900	$5050
c Other income	$2000	$950	$101
Deflator for a, b, c	1.0	1.26	1.10
Input			
a Labour	$800	$3000	$750
Deflator	1.0	1.15	1.14
b Material	$400	$720	$375
Deflator	1.0	1.12	1.11
c Capital	$350	$402	$380
Deflator	1.0	1.16	1.18
d Energy	$120	$159	$109
Deflator	1.0	1.09	1.14
e Robotic expense	$284	$420	$210
Deflator	1.0	1.10	1.12
f Computer expense	$100	$120	$102
Deflator	1.0	1.13	1.16
g Administrative expense	$200	$402	$207
Deflator	1.0	1.16	1.18
h Other expenses	$95	$201	$100
Deflator	1.0	1.17	1.14

Question 14 Estimate the mean and standard deviation of the insurance claims process. The observations listed below reflect the defective claims. Also estimate the process capability.

101	107	98	113	103
171	181	29	41	99
20	41	47	103	105
104	111	101	97	98

Question 15 Find the capability limits of a tool making process which is approximately normally distributed if the means and ranges of the subgroups of size 4 are as follows:

Chart	Sub group			
	1	2	3	4
$\bar{x}$	151	153	147	139
R	12	10	10	15

Question 16 Calculate the trail control limits and centre line for a percentage chart based on the following data obtained from a secretarial typing pool.

Number of subgroups inspected	=	45
Subgroup size	=	100
Total number of defectives	=	135

Question 17 What is meant by the terms quality at the source and productivity at the source? How would you define the quality that the customer sees?

Question 18 Define the terms consumer's risk and producer's risk?

Question 19 Why are inspection and testing processes classified as non-value adding operations?

Question 20 The general postmaster at West Valley wishes to implement a productivity and quality programme but does not know how to proceed. Outline the steps that the general postmaster should follow in order to be successful in his objectives.

Question 21 The defect rate of a clinical operation at Hoyer Hospital is 35%. The manager of the clinical operations says 25% of the defects are due to poor incoming materials. The supplier of the incoming materials believes his process is perfect. The hospital unit is losing patients at the rate of 216 per day. Develop a comprehensive productivity and quality improvement process that will enable Hoyer Hospital to be competitive, reduce defect levels to zero and regain patient confidence and business.

Question 22 Is zero defect achievable? Why or why not?

Question 23 Crosby says quality is free. Do you agree with this statement? Why or why not?

Question 24 Explain how the morale and motivation level of individuals can affect productivity and quality.

Question 25 Edosomwan proposes that 80% of productivity and quality errors that occur in the manufacturing and service work environments are due to management mistakes. Do you agree with this statement? Why or why not? Develop improving strategies for minimising management mistakes that affect the level of productivity growth and quality improvement.

Question 26 Discuss the major requirements typical senior management of a company look for when reviewing productivity and quality improvement projects.

Question 27 Why do people resist change?

Question 28 The output temperature from a computer power supply is assumed to be normally distributed. Twenty observations taken over a period of twenty days are presented below:

90	87	89	92	93
88	95	91	87	94
85	89	90	95	80
87	83	82	81	96

a Calculate the mean and standard deviation of the data presented.
b Construct a 95% two-sided confidence interval on mean and on variance.

Question 29 A random sample of 400 printed circuit boards contains 50 defective units. Construct a 95% two-sided confidence interval on the process fraction defective.

Question 30 The manager of Johnson Computer Company wishes to test the hypothesis

Null hypothesis (H_π): mean $(\mu = 25)$
Alternative hypothesis (H_π): mean $(\mu = 25)$

The variance of the population is 7.0, the true mean is 28. Calculate the appropriate sample size (n) that the manager should use to ensure that the probability of type II error is not greater than 20%. Assume that the probability for committing a type I error is 0.10.

Question 31 Develop a step-by-step approach for dealing with resistance to change when implementing new productivity and quality improvement ideas.

Question 32 Why are 3-sigma limits used in control charts? When is it appropriate to use 2-sigma and 1-sigma limits on control charts?

Question 33 When a process is in a state of statistical control, is it possible to find defective output? Why or why not?

Question 34 Develop a step-by-step procedure for searching for assignable causes when a process is not in a state of statistical process control.

Question 35 Identify the various costs of quality and present ideas on how they can be controlled and minimised in a manufacturing environment and b service environment.

Question 36 A control chart for fraction defective indicates that the current process average is 0.45. The sample size is constant at 300 units. a Calculate the 2-sigma control limits for the control chart; b calculate the 3-sigma control limits for the control chart.

Question 37 Suppose the following data are presented for the U and C charts: $C = 8$, $n = 8$, process average equal 6 defectives. Calculate the upper and lower control limits for both the U and the C charts.

Question 38 How would you go about justifying a potential statistical process control and productivity improvement project? What are the key dependencies that must be addressed before you can proceed with SPC implementation?

Question 39 Inspection and testing process have no value to the final output produced. Do you agree with the above statement? Why or why not? What types of inspection or testing process would you recommend to a manufacturing manager who is trying to resolve a chronic quality problem from a supplier.

Question 40 How would you go about enhancing the teamwork between supplier, process owner, and customer? Identify some of the key problems involved in dealing with suppliers and customers.

Question 41 Is zero inventory achievable? Why or why not?

Question 42 Define just-in-time productivity and quality improvement at the source. What are some of the problems involved when implementing JIT in a manufacturing environment with large lot sizes and frequent set-up.

Question 43 What is the impact of process changes on statistical process control? How should a new process be introduced into existing ones to minimise interruption?

Question 44 What are the roles of senior managers, project managers and engineers in balancing productivity and quality objectives? Develop a resource allocation scheme that permits equal attention to productivity and quality improvement projects.

Question 45 How do the following affect the level of productivity improvement and quality:

a Employee morale.

b Work design and task layout.

c Equipment and tool safety.

d Human factors such as noise level.

e Managerial leadership style.

f Company compensation and reward structure.

Question 46 Why is it dangerous to rely on partial measures of productivity, such as labour productivity?

Question 47 Under what circumstances should one change the base period when measuring productivity at any level?

Question 48 How would you go about convincing a manufacturing manager to build quality into the product and not to inspect quality into the product?

Question 49 Discuss some of the difficulties involved in controlling the cost of quality and the cost of productivity improvement.

Question 50 Explain the differences between product specification limits and statistical process control limits for controlling the same product quality.

APPENDIX B: PRODUCTIVITY AND QUALITY IMPROVEMENT TABLES, WORK FORMS AND STATISTICAL FORMULAE

Acknowledgement

Control Chart Formulas and Work Forms and Tables are adapted from Process Control, Capability and Improvement. The IBM Quality Institute Publication, Southbury, Connecticut, May 1985, Reprinted with Permission.
Constant Formulas for Control Charts adapted from ASTM Publication STP-15D, Manual on the Presentation of Data Control and Analysis, 1976, pp. 134-136 Copyright ASTM, 1916. Race Street, Philadelphia, Pennsylvania 19103, Reprinted with permission.

Statistical tables

Standard normal distribution (area under normal curve)

a = the proportion of process output beyond a particular value of interest (such as a specification limit) that is z standard deviation units away from the process average (for a process that is in statistical control and is normally distributed). For example, if z = 2.17, a = .0150 or 1.5% . In any actual situation, this proportion is only approximate.

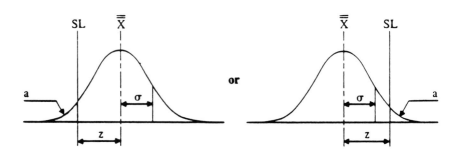

|z|	x.x0	x.x1	x.x2	x.x3	x.x4	x.x5	x.x6	x.x7	x.x8	x.x9
4.0	.00003									
3.9	.00005	.00005	.00004	.00004	.00004	.00004	.00004	.00004	.00003	.00003
3.8	.00007	.00007	.00007	.00006	.00006	.00006	.00006	.00005	.00005	.00005
3.7	.00011	.00010	.00010	.00010	.00009	.00009	.00008	.00008	.00008	.00008
3.6	.00016	.00015	.00015	.00014	.00014	.00013	.00013	.00012	.00012	.00011
3.5	.00023	.00022	.00022	.00021	.00020	.00019	.00019	.00018	.00017	.00017
3.4	.00034	.00032	.00031	.00030	.00029	.00028	.00027	.00026	.00025	.00024
3.3	.00048	.00047	.00045	.00043	.00042	.00040	.00039	.00038	.00036	.00035
3.2	.00069	.00066	.00064	.00062	.00060	.00058	.00056	.00054	.00052	.00050
3.1	.00097	.00094	.00090	.00087	.00084	.00082	.00079	.00076	.00074	.00071
3.0	.00135	.00131	.00126	.00122	.00118	.00114	.00111	.00107	.00104	.00100
2.9	.0019	.0018	.0018	.0017	.0016	.0016	.0015	.0015	.0014	.0014
2.8	.0026	.0025	.0024	.0023	.0023	.0022	.0021	.0021	.0020	.0019
2.7	.0035	.0034	.0033	.0032	.0031	.0030	.0029	.0028	.0027	.0026
2.6	.0047	.0045	.0044	.0043	.0041	.0040	.0039	.0038	.0037	.0036
2.5	.0062	.0060	.0059	.0057	.0055	.0054	.0052	.0051	.0049	.0048
2.4	.0082	.0080	.0078	.0075	.0073	.0071	.0069	.0068	.0066	.0064
2.3	.0107	.0104	.0102	.0099	.0096	.0094	.0091	.0089	.0087	.0084
2.2	.0139	.0136	.0132	.0129	.0125	.0122	.0119	.0116	.0113	.0110
2.1	.0179	.0174	.0170	.0166	.0162	.0158	.0154	.0150	.0146	.0143
2.0	.0228	.0222	.0217	.0212	.0207	.0202	.0197	.0192	.0188	.0183
1.9	.0287	.0281	.0274	.0268	.0262	.0256	.0250	.0244	.0239	.0233
1.8	.0359	.0351	.0344	.0336	.0329	.0322	.0314	.0307	.0301	.0294
1.7	.0446	.0436	.0427	.0418	.0409	.0401	.0392	.0384	.0375	.0367
1.6	.0548	.0537	.0526	.0516	.0505	.0495	.0485	.0475	.0465	.0455
1.5	.0668	.0655	.0643	.0630	.0618	.0606	.0594	.0582	.0571	.0559
1.4	.0808	.0793	.0778	.0764	.0749	.0735	.0721	.0708	.0694	.0681
1.3	.0968	.0951	.0934	.0918	.0901	.0885	.0869	.0853	.0838	.0823
1.2	.1151	.1131	.1112	.1093	.1075	.1056	.1038	.1020	.1003	.0985
1.1	.1357	.1335	.1314	.1292	.1271	.1251	.1230	.1210	.1190	.1170
1.0	.1587	.1562	.1539	.1515	.1492	.1469	.1446	.1423	.1401	.1379
0.9	.1841	.1814	.1788	.1762	.1736	.1711	.1685	.1660	.1635	.1611
0.8	.2119	.2090	.2061	.2033	.2005	.1977	.1949	.1922	.1894	.1867
0.7	.2420	.2389	.2358	.2327	.2297	.2266	.2236	.2206	.2177	.2148
0.6	.2743	.2709	.2676	.2643	.2611	.2578	.2546	.2514	.2483	.2451
0.5	.3085	.3050	.3015	.2981	.2946	.2912	.2877	.2843	.2810	.2776
0.4	.3446	.3409	.3372	.3336	.3300	.3264	.3228	.3192	.3156	.3121
0.3	.3821	.3783	.3745	.3707	.3669	.3632	.3594	.3557	.3520	.3483
0.2	.4207	.4168	.4129	.4090	.4052	.4013	.3974	.3936	.3897	.3859
0.1	.4602	.4562	.4522	.4483	.4443	.4404	.4364	.4325	.4286	.4247
0.0	.5000	.4960	.4920	.4880	.4840	.4801	.4761	.4721	.4681	.4641

F-distribution table, $\alpha = 0.5$

d.f.2 (denominator)	d.f.1 (numerator)																		
	1	2	3	4	5	6	7	8	9	10	12	15	20	24	30	40	60	120	∞
1	161	200	216	225	230	234	237	239	241	242	244	246	248	249	250	251	252	253	254
2	18.5	19.0	19.2	19.2	19.3	19.3	19.4	19.4	19.4	19.4	19.4	19.4	19.4	19.5	19.5	19.5	19.5	19.5	19.5
3	10.1	9.55	9.28	9.12	9.01	8.94	8.89	8.85	8.81	8.79	8.74	8.70	8.66	8.64	8.62	8.59	8.57	8.55	8.53
4	7.71	6.94	6.59	6.39	6.26	6.16	6.09	6.04	6.00	5.96	5.91	5.86	5.80	5.77	5.75	5.72	5.69	5.66	5.63
5	6.61	5.79	5.41	5.19	5.05	4.95	4.88	4.82	4.77	4.74	4.68	4.62	4.56	4.53	4.50	4.46	4.43	4.40	4.37
6	5.99	5.14	4.76	4.53	4.39	4.28	4.21	4.15	4.10	4.06	4.00	3.94	3.87	3.84	3.81	3.77	3.74	3.70	3.67
7	5.59	4.74	4.35	4.12	3.97	3.87	3.79	3.73	3.68	3.64	3.57	3.51	3.44	3.41	3.38	3.34	3.30	3.27	3.23
8	5.32	4.46	4.07	3.84	3.69	3.58	3.50	3.44	3.39	3.35	3.28	3.22	3.15	3.12	3.08	3.04	3.01	2.97	2.93
9	5.12	4.26	3.86	3.63	3.48	3.37	3.29	3.23	3.18	3.14	3.07	3.01	2.94	2.90	2.86	2.83	2.79	2.75	2.71
10	4.96	4.10	3.71	3.48	3.33	3.22	3.14	3.07	3.02	2.98	2.91	2.85	2.77	2.74	2.70	2.66	2.62	2.58	2.54
11	4.84	3.98	3.59	3.36	3.20	3.09	3.01	2.95	2.90	2.85	2.79	2.72	2.65	2.61	2.57	2.53	2.49	2.45	2.40
12	4.75	3.89	3.49	3.26	3.11	3.00	2.91	2.85	2.80	2.75	2.69	2.62	2.54	2.51	2.47	2.43	2.38	2.34	2.30
13	4.67	3.81	3.41	3.18	3.03	2.92	2.83	2.77	2.71	2.67	2.60	2.53	2.46	2.42	2.38	2.34	2.30	2.25	2.21
14	4.60	3.74	3.34	3.11	2.96	2.85	2.76	2.70	2.65	2.60	2.53	2.46	2.39	2.35	2.31	2.27	2.22	2.18	2.13
15	4.54	3.68	3.29	3.06	2.90	2.79	2.71	2.64	2.59	2.54	2.48	2.40	2.33	2.29	2.25	2.20	2.16	2.11	2.07
16	4.49	3.63	3.24	3.01	2.85	2.74	2.66	2.59	2.54	2.49	2.42	2.35	2.28	2.24	2.19	2.15	2.11	2.06	2.01
17	4.45	3.59	3.20	2.96	2.81	2.70	2.61	2.55	2.49	2.45	2.38	2.31	2.23	2.19	2.15	2.10	2.06	2.01	1.96
18	4.41	3.55	3.16	2.93	2.77	2.66	2.58	2.51	2.46	2.41	2.34	2.27	2.19	2.15	2.11	2.06	2.02	1.97	1.92
19	4.38	3.52	3.13	2.90	2.74	2.63	2.54	2.48	2.42	2.38	2.31	2.23	2.16	2.11	2.07	2.03	1.98	1.93	1.88
20	4.35	3.49	3.10	2.87	2.71	2.60	2.51	2.45	2.39	2.35	2.28	2.20	2.12	2.08	2.04	1.99	1.95	1.90	1.84
21	4.32	3.47	3.07	2.84	2.68	2.57	2.49	2.42	2.37	2.32	2.25	2.18	2.10	2.05	2.01	1.96	1.92	1.87	1.81
22	4.30	3.44	3.05	2.82	2.66	2.55	2.46	2.40	2.34	2.30	2.23	2.15	2.07	2.03	1.98	1.94	1.89	1.84	1.78
23	4.28	3.42	3.03	2.80	2.64	2.53	2.44	2.37	2.32	2.27	2.20	2.13	2.05	2.01	1.96	1.91	1.86	1.81	1.76
24	4.26	3.40	3.01	2.78	2.62	2.51	2.42	2.36	2.30	2.25	2.18	2.11	2.03	1.98	1.94	1.89	1.84	1.79	1.73
25	4.24	3.39	2.99	2.76	2.60	2.49	2.40	2.34	2.28	2.24	2.16	2.09	2.01	1.96	1.92	1.87	1.82	1.77	1.71
30	4.17	3.32	2.92	2.69	2.53	2.42	2.33	2.27	2.21	2.16	2.09	2.01	1.93	1.89	1.84	1.79	1.74	1.68	1.62
40	4.08	3.23	2.84	2.61	2.45	2.34	2.25	2.18	2.12	2.08	2.00	1.92	1.84	1.79	1.74	1.69	1.64	1.58	1.51
60	4.00	3.15	2.76	2.53	2.37	2.25	2.17	2.10	2.04	1.99	1.92	1.84	1.75	1.70	1.65	1.59	1.53	1.47	1.39
120	3.92	3.07	2.68	2.45	2.29	2.18	2.09	2.02	1.96	1.91	1.83	1.75	1.66	1.61	1.55	1.50	1.43	1.35	1.25
∞	3.84	3.00	2.60	2.37	2.21	2.10	2.01	1.94	1.88	1.83	1.75	1.67	1.57	1.52	1.46	1.39	1.32	1.22	1.00

F-distribution table, α = 0.01

d.f.2 (denom-inator)	1	2	3	4	5	6	7	8	9	10	12	15	20	24	30	40	60	120	∞
1	4,052	5,000	5,403	5,625	5,764	5,859	5,928	5,982	6,023	6,056	6,106	6,157	6,209	6,235	6,261	6,287	6,313	6,339	6,366
2	98.5	99.0	99.2	99.2	99.3	99.3	99.4	99.4	99.4	99.4	99.4	99.4	99.4	99.5	99.5	99.5	99.5	99.5	99.5
3	34.1	30.8	29.5	28.7	28.2	27.9	27.7	27.5	27.3	27.2	27.1	26.9	26.7	26.6	26.5	26.4	26.3	26.2	26.1
4	21.2	18.0	16.7	16.0	15.5	15.2	15.0	14.8	14.7	14.5	14.4	14.2	14.0	13.9	13.8	13.7	13.7	13.6	13.5
5	16.3	13.3	12.1	11.4	11.0	10.7	10.5	10.3	10.2	10.1	9.89	9.72	9.55	9.47	9.38	9.29	9.20	9.11	9.02
6	13.7	10.9	9.78	9.15	8.75	8.47	8.26	8.10	7.98	7.87	7.72	7.56	7.40	7.31	7.23	7.14	7.06	6.97	6.88
7	12.2	9.55	8.45	7.85	7.46	7.19	6.99	6.84	6.72	6.62	6.47	6.31	6.16	6.07	5.99	5.91	5.82	5.74	5.65
8	11.3	8.65	7.59	7.01	6.63	6.37	6.18	6.03	5.91	5.81	5.67	5.52	5.36	5.28	5.20	5.12	5.03	4.95	4.86
9	10.6	8.02	6.99	6.42	6.06	5.80	5.61	5.47	5.35	5.26	5.11	4.96	4.81	4.73	4.65	4.57	4.48	4.40	4.31
10	10.0	7.56	6.55	5.99	5.64	5.39	5.20	5.06	4.94	4.85	4.71	4.56	4.41	4.33	4.25	4.17	4.08	4.00	3.91
11	9.65	7.21	6.22	5.67	5.32	5.07	4.89	4.74	4.63	4.54	4.40	4.25	4.10	4.02	3.94	3.86	3.78	3.69	3.60
12	9.33	6.93	5.95	5.41	5.06	4.82	4.64	4.50	4.39	4.30	4.16	4.01	3.86	3.78	3.70	3.62	3.54	3.45	3.36
13	9.07	6.70	5.74	5.21	4.86	4.62	4.44	4.30	4.19	4.10	3.96	3.82	3.66	3.59	3.51	3.43	3.34	3.25	3.17
14	8.86	6.51	5.56	5.04	4.70	4.46	4.28	4.14	4.03	3.94	3.80	3.66	3.51	3.43	3.35	3.27	3.18	3.09	3.00
15	8.68	6.36	5.42	4.89	4.56	4.32	4.14	4.00	3.89	3.80	3.67	3.52	3.37	3.29	3.21	3.13	3.05	2.96	2.87
16	8.53	6.23	5.29	4.77	4.44	4.20	4.03	3.89	3.78	3.69	3.55	3.41	3.26	3.18	3.10	3.02	2.93	2.84	2.75
17	8.40	6.11	5.19	4.67	4.34	4.10	3.93	3.79	3.68	3.59	3.46	3.31	3.16	3.08	3.00	2.92	2.83	2.75	2.65
18	8.29	6.01	5.09	4.58	4.25	4.01	3.84	3.71	3.60	3.51	3.37	3.23	3.08	3.00	2.92	2.84	2.75	2.66	2.57
19	8.19	5.93	5.01	4.50	4.17	3.94	3.77	3.63	3.52	3.43	3.30	3.15	3.00	2.92	2.84	2.76	2.67	2.58	2.49
20	8.10	5.85	4.94	4.43	4.10	3.87	3.70	3.56	3.46	3.37	3.23	3.09	2.94	2.86	2.78	2.69	2.61	2.52	2.42
21	8.02	5.78	4.87	4.37	4.04	3.81	3.64	3.51	3.40	3.31	3.17	3.03	2.88	2.80	2.72	2.64	2.55	2.46	2.36
22	7.95	5.72	4.82	4.31	3.99	3.76	3.59	3.45	3.35	3.26	3.12	2.98	2.83	2.75	2.67	2.58	2.50	2.40	2.31
23	7.88	5.66	4.76	4.26	3.94	3.71	3.54	3.41	3.30	3.21	3.07	2.93	2.78	2.70	2.62	2.54	2.45	2.35	2.26
24	7.82	5.61	4.72	4.22	3.90	3.67	3.50	3.36	3.26	3.17	3.03	2.89	2.74	2.66	2.58	2.49	2.40	2.31	2.21
25	7.77	5.57	4.68	4.18	3.86	3.63	3.46	3.32	3.22	3.13	2.99	2.85	2.70	2.62	2.53	2.45	2.36	2.27	2.17
30	7.56	5.39	4.51	4.02	3.70	3.47	3.30	3.17	3.07	2.98	2.84	2.70	2.55	2.47	2.39	2.30	2.21	2.11	2.01
40	7.31	5.18	4.31	3.83	3.51	3.29	3.12	2.99	2.89	2.80	2.66	2.52	2.37	2.29	2.20	2.11	2.02	1.92	1.80
60	7.08	4.98	4.13	3.65	3.34	3.12	2.95	2.82	2.72	2.63	2.50	2.35	2.20	2.12	2.03	1.94	1.84	1.73	1.60
120	6.85	4.79	3.95	3.48	3.17	2.96	2.79	2.66	2.56	2.47	2.34	2.19	2.03	1.95	1.86	1.76	1.66	1.53	1.38
∞	6.63	4.61	3.78	3.32	3.02	2.80	2.64	2.51	2.41	2.32	2.18	2.04	1.88	1.79	1.70	1.59	1.47	1.32	1.00

d.f.1 (numerator)

Percentage points of the χ^2 distribution[a]

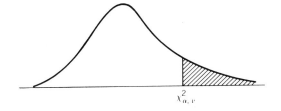

				α					
ν	0.995	0.990	0.975	0.950	0.500	0.050	0.025	0.010	0.005
1	0.00 +	0.00 +	0.00 +	0.00 +	0.45	3.84	5.02	6.63	7.88
2	0.01	0.02	0.05	0.10	1.39	5.99	7.38	9.21	10.60
3	0.07	0.11	0.22	0.35	2.37	7.81	9.35	11.34	12.84
4	0.21	0.30	0.48	0.71	3.36	9.49	11.14	13.28	14.86
5	0.41	0.55	0.83	1.15	4.35	11.07	12.38	15.09	16.75
6	0.68	0.87	1.24	1.64	5.35	12.59	14.45	16.81	18.55
7	0·99	1.24	1.69	2.17	6.35	14.07	16.01	18.48	20.28
8	1.34	1.65	2.18	2.73	7.34	15.51	17.53	20.09	21.96
9	1.73	2.09	2.70	3.33	8.34	16.92	19.02	21.67	23.59
10	2.16	2.56	3.25	3.94	9.34	18.31	20.48	23.21	25.19
11	2.60	3.05	3.82	4.57	10.34	19.68	21.92	24.72	26.76
12	3.07	3.57	4.40	5.23	11.34	21.03	23.34	26.22	28.30
13	3.57	4.11	5.01	5.89	12.34	22.36	24.74	27.69	29.82
14	4.07	4.66	5.63	6.57	13.34	23.68	26.12	29.14	31.32
15	4.60	5.23	6.27	7.26	14.34	25.00	27.49	30.58	32.80
16	5.14	5.81	6.91	7.96	15.34	26.30	28.85	32.00	34.27
17	5.70	6.41	7.56	8.67	16.34	27.59	30.19	33.41	35.72
18	6.26	7.01	8.23	9.39	17.34	28.87	31.53	34.81	37.16
19	6.84	7.63	8.91	10.12	18.34	30.14	32.85	36.19	38.58
20	7.43	8.26	9.59	10.85	19.34	31.41	34.17	37.57	40.00
25	10.52	11.52	13.12	14.61	24.34	37.65	40.65	44.31	46.93
30	13.79	14.95	16.79	18.49	29.34	43.77	46.98	50.89	53.67
40	20.71	22.16	24.43	26.51	39.34	55.76	59.34	63.69	66.77
50	27.99	29.71	32.36	34.76	49.33	67.50	71.42	76.15	79.49
60	35.53	37.48	40.48	43.19	59.33	79.08	83.30	88.38	91.95
70	43.28	45.44	48.76	51.74	69.33	90.53	95.02	100.42	104.22
80	51.17	53.54	57.15	60.39	79.33	101.88	106.63	112.33	116.32
90	59.20	61.75	65.65	69.13	89.33	113.14	118.14	124.12	128.30
100	67.33	70.06	74.22	77.93	99.33	124.34	129.56	135.81	140.17

ν = degrees of freedom.
[a] Adapted with permission from *Biometrika Tables for Statisticians*, Vol. 1, 3rd ed., by E. S. Pearson and H. O. Hartley, Cambridge University Press, Cambridge, 1966.

t-distribution table

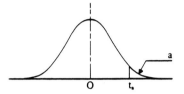

d.f.	$t_{.100}$	$t_{.050}$	$t_{.025}$	$t_{.010}$	$t_{.005}$
1	3.078	6.314	12.706	31.821	63.657
2	1.886	2.920	4.303	6.965	9.925
3	1.638	2.353	3.182	4.541	5.841
4	1.533	2.132	2.776	3.747	4.604
5	1.476	2.015	2.571	3.365	4.032
6	1.440	1.943	2.447	3.143	3.707
7	1.415	1.895	2.365	2.998	3.499
8	1.397	1.860	2.306	2.896	3.355
9	1.383	1.833	2.262	2.821	3.250
10	1.372	1.812	2.228	2.764	3.169
11	1.363	1.796	2.201	2.718	3.106
12	1.356	1.782	2.179	2.681	3.055
13	1.350	1.771	2.160	2.650	3.012
14	1.345	1.761	2.145	2.624	2.977
15	1.341	1.753	2.131	2.602	2.947
16	1.337	1.746	2.120	2.583	2.921
17	1.333	1.740	2.110	2.567	2.898
18	1.330	1.734	2.101	2.552	2.878
19	1.328	1.729	2.093	2.539	2.861
20	1.325	1.725	2.086	2.528	2.845
21	1.323	1.721	2.080	2.518	2.831
22	1.321	1.717	2.074	2.508	2.819
23	1.319	1.714	2.069	2.500	2.807
24	1.318	1.711	2.064	2.492	2.797
25	1.316	1.708	2.060	2.485	2.787
26	1.315	1.706	2.056	2.479	2.779
27	1.314	1.703	2.052	2.473	2.771
28	1.313	1.701	2.048	2.467	2.763
29	1.311	1.699	2.045	2.462	2.756
∞	1.282	1.645	1.960	2.326	2.576

Instruments for constructing control charts

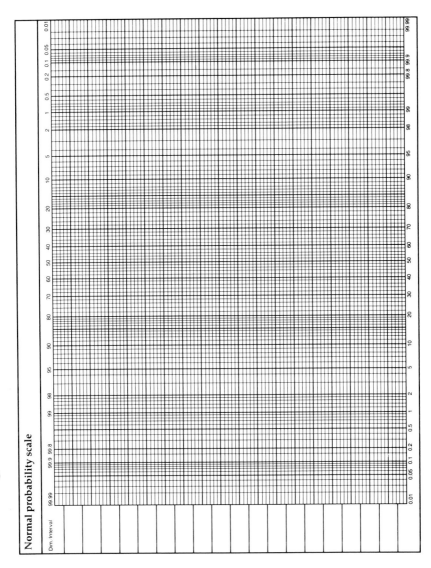

Statistical process control histogram

Part Asm. Name		Machine		Operation Type:		Nominal	
Part No.		Brass Tag No.		☐ Sub. Asm.		Upper Spec. Limit	
Parameter		Tool No.		☐ Sub. Asm. Test		Lower Spec. Limit	
Operation		Start Date		☐ Final Asm.		Gaging Method	
Department		End Date		☐ Final Test		Unit of Measure	
				☐ Other		Sample Frequency	

Dim.	5	10	15	20	25	30	35	40	45	No.	%	Cum. %

Operators

Sketch of Dimension

Total

Variables control chart X̄ and R (averages and ranges)

Part/Asm. Name	Operation	Specification	Chart No.
Part No.	Department	Gage	Unit of Measure
Parameter	Machine	Sample Size/Frequency	Zero Equals

Date																									
Time																									
Operator																									
Sample Measurements 1																									
2																									
3																									
4																									
5																									
Sum																									
Average X̄																									
Range R																									

Averages

Ranges

Variables control chart X̄ and R (averages and ranges) calculation worksheet

Preliminary Control Limits (based on subgroups: _____)	**Revised Control Limits** (if necessary)
Calculate Average Range: $\bar{R} = \dfrac{\Sigma R}{k} =$ _____ = _____ Σ = Sum of, and k = number of subgroups **Calculate Control Limits for Ranges:** $UCL_R = D_4 \times \bar{R} =$ _____ × _____ = _____ $LCL_R = D_3 \times \bar{R} =$ _____ × _____ = _____	$\bar{R} =$ _____ = _____ $UCL_R =$ _____ × _____ = _____ $LCL_R =$ _____ × _____ = _____
Calculate Grand Average: $\bar{\bar{X}} = \dfrac{\Sigma \bar{X}}{k} =$ _____ = _____ **Calculate Control Limits for Averages:** $A_2\bar{R} =$ _____ × _____ = _____ $UCL_{\bar{X}} = \bar{\bar{X}} + A_2\bar{R} =$ _____ + _____ = _____ $LCL_{\bar{X}} = \bar{\bar{X}} - A_2\bar{R} =$ _____ − _____ = _____	$\bar{\bar{X}} =$ _____ = _____ $A_2\bar{R} =$ _____ × _____ = _____ $UCL_{\bar{X}} =$ _____ + _____ = _____ $LCL_{\bar{X}} =$ _____ − _____ = _____

Estimate of Standard Deviation (If the process is in statistical control):

$\sigma = \dfrac{\bar{R}}{d_2} =$ _____

Subgroup Size n	A_2	D_3	D_4	d_2	Subgroup Size n	A_2	D_3	D_4	d_2
2	1.880	*	3.267	1.128	6	0.483	*	2.004	2.534
3	1.023	*	2.575	1.693	7	0.419	0.076	1.924	2.704
4	0.729	*	2.282	2.059	8	0.373	0.136	1.864	2.847
5	0.577	*	2.115	2.326	9	0.337	0.184	1.816	2.970
					10	0.308	0.223	1.777	3.078

*Lower control limits for R do not exist for sample sizes below 7.

Notes: Record all adjustments, tool changes, etc.

Subgroup No.	Date	Time	Comments

Variables control chart X̄ and S (average and sample standard deviations)

Part/Asm. Name	Operation	Specification	Chart No.
Part No.	Department	Gage	Unit of Measure
Parameter	Machine	Sampling Frequency	Zero Equals

Date											
Time											
Operator											
Sample Size											
Average X̄											
Std. Dev. S											

Averages

Standard Deviations

Variables control chart $\bar{X}$ and S (average and sample standard deviations) calculation worksheet

Calculate Average Standard Deviation:

$$\bar{S} = \frac{\Sigma S}{k} = \underline{\hspace{1.5cm}} = \underline{\hspace{1.5cm}}$$

where Σ = sum of, and k = number of subgroups

Calculate Control Limits for Standard Deviation:

$UCL_s = B_4 \times \bar{S} = \underline{\hspace{1.5cm}} \times \underline{\hspace{1.5cm}} = \underline{\hspace{1.5cm}}$

$LCL_s = B_3 \times \bar{S} = \underline{\hspace{1.5cm}} \times \underline{\hspace{1.5cm}} = \underline{\hspace{1.5cm}}$

Calculate Grand Averages:

$$\bar{\bar{X}} = \frac{\Sigma \bar{X}}{k} = \underline{\hspace{1.5cm}} = \underline{\hspace{1.5cm}}$$

Calculate Control Limits for Averages:

$A_3\bar{S} = \underline{\hspace{1.5cm}} \times \underline{\hspace{1.5cm}} = \underline{\hspace{1.5cm}}$

$UCL_{\bar{X}} = \bar{\bar{X}} + A_3\bar{S} = \underline{\hspace{1.5cm}} + \underline{\hspace{1.5cm}} = \underline{\hspace{1.5cm}}$

$LCL_{\bar{X}} = \bar{\bar{X}} - A_3\bar{S} = \underline{\hspace{1.5cm}} - \underline{\hspace{1.5cm}} = \underline{\hspace{1.5cm}}$

Estimate of Process Standard Deviation:
(If the process is in statistical control)

$\hat{\sigma} = \bar{S}/c_4 = \underline{\hspace{1.5cm}} = \underline{\hspace{1.5cm}}$

Subgroup Size n	A_3	B_3	B_4	c_4	Subgroup Size n	A_3	B_3	B_4	c_4
2	2.659	*	3.267	0.7979	16	0.763	0.448	1.552	0.9835
3	1.954	*	2.568	0.8862	17	0.739	0.466	1.534	0.9845
4	1.628	*	2.266	0.9213	18	0.718	0.482	1.518	0.9854
5	1.427	*	2.089	0.9400	19	0.698	0.497	1.503	0.9862
6	1.287	0.030	1.970	0.9515	20	0.680	0.510	1.490	0.9869
7	1.182	0.118	1.882	0.9594	21	0.663	0.523	1.477	0.9876
8	1.099	0.185	1.815	0.9650	22	0.647	0.534	1.466	0.9882
9	1.032	0.239	1.761	0.9693	23	0.633	0.545	1.455	0.9887
10	0.975	0.284	1.716	0.9727	24	0.619	0.555	1.445	0.9892
11	0.927	0.321	1.679	0.9754	25	0.606	0.565	1.435	0.9896
12	0.886	0.354	1.646	0.9776					
13	0.850	0.382	1.618	0.9794					
14	0.817	0.406	1.594	0.9810					
15	0.789	0.428	1.572	0.9823					

*There is no lower control limit for standard deviations for sample sizes below 6.

Notes: Record all adjustments, tool changes, etc.

Subgroup No.	Date	Time	Comments

Variables control chart for medians X̄ and R (medians and ranges)

Part/Asm. Name	Operation	Specification	Chart No.
Part No	Department	Gage	Unit of Measure
Parameter	Machine	Sample Size/Frequency	Zero Equals

Date				
Time				
Operator				

Sample Measurements	1
	2
	3
	4
	5

Sum	
Median X̄	
Range R	

Medians

Ranges

Variables control chart for medians $\tilde{X}$ and R (medians and ranges) calculation worksheet

Preliminary Control Limits (based on subgroups: _____)	Revised Control Limits (if necessary)

Calculate Average Range:

$\bar{R} = \dfrac{\Sigma R}{k} =$ _____ = _____

$\Sigma =$ Sum of, and $k =$ number of subgroups

$\bar{R} =$ _____ = _____

Calculate Control Limits for Ranges:

$UCL_R = D_4 \times \bar{R} =$ _____ $\times$ _____ = _____

$LCL_R = D_3 \times \bar{R} =$ _____ $\times$ _____ = _____

$UCL_R =$ _____ $\times$ _____ = _____

$LCL_R =$ _____ $\times$ _____ = _____

Calculate Average of Medians:

$\bar{\bar{X}} = \dfrac{\tilde{X}}{k} =$ _____ = _____

$\bar{\bar{X}} =$ _____ = _____

Calculate Control Limits for Medians:

$\bar{A}_2 \bar{R} =$ _____ $\times$ _____ = _____

$UCL = \bar{\bar{X}} + \bar{A}_2 \bar{R} =$ _____ + _____ = _____

$LCL = \bar{\bar{X}} - \bar{A}_2 \bar{R} =$ _____ - _____ = _____

$\bar{A}_2 \bar{R} =$ _____ $\times$ _____ = _____

$UCL_x =$ _____ + _____ = _____

$LCL_x =$ _____ - _____ = _____

Estimate of Standard Deviation (If the process is in statistical control):

$\sigma = \dfrac{\bar{R}}{d_2} =$ _____ ___

Subgroup Size n	$\bar{A}_2$	D_3	D_4	d_2	Subgroup Size n	$\bar{A}_2$	D_3	D_4	d_2
2	1.88	*	3.267	1.128	6	0.55	*	2.004	2.534
3	1.19	*	2.575	1.693	7	0.51	0.076	1.924	2.704
4	0.80	*	2.282	2.059	8	0.43	0.136	1.864	2.847
5	0.69	*	2.115	2.326	9	0.41	0.184	1.816	2.970
					10	0.36	0.223	1.777	3.078

*Lower control limits for R do not exist for sample sizes below 7.

Notes: Record all adjustments, tool changes, etc.

Subgroup No.	Date	Time	Comments

Variables control chart for individuals X and R (individuals and ranges)

Part/Asm. Name	Operation	Specification	Chart No
Part No	Department	Gage	Unit of Measure
Parameter	Machine	Sample Size/Frequency	Zero Equals

	1	2	3	4	5	6	7	8	9	10	11	12	13	14	15	16	17	18	19	20	21	22	23	24	25
Date																									
Time																									
Operator																									
Sum																									
Average X̄																									
Moving Range																									

Individuals

Moving Ranges

Variables control chart for individuals X and R (individuals and ranges) calculation worksheet

Preliminary Control Limits (based on subgroups: _____)	Revised Control Limits (if necessary)
Calculate Average Range: $\bar{R} = \dfrac{\Sigma R}{k}$ = _____ = _____ Σ = Sum of, and k = number of subgroups **Calculate Control Limits for Ranges:** $UCL_R = D_4 \times \bar{R}$ = _____ x _____ = _____ $LCL_R = D_3 \times \bar{R}$ = _____ x _____ = _____	$\bar{R}$ = _____ = _____ UCL_R = _____ x _____ = _____ LCL_R = _____ x _____ = _____
Calculate Process Average: $\bar{X} = \dfrac{\Sigma X}{k}$ = _____ = _____ **Calculate Control Limits for Individuals:** $E_2\bar{R}$ = _____ x _____ = _____ $UCL_x = \bar{X} + E_2\bar{R}$ = _____ + _____ = _____ $LCL_x = \bar{X} - E_2\bar{R}$ = _____ - _____ = _____	$\bar{X}$ = _____ = _____ $E_2\bar{R}$ = _____ x _____ = _____ UCL_x = _____ + _____ = _____ LCL_x = _____ - _____ = _____

Estimate of Standard Deviation (If the process is in statistical control):

$\hat{\sigma} = \dfrac{\bar{R}}{d_2}$ = _____

Subgroup Size					Subgroup Size				
n	E_2	D_3	D_4	d_2	n	E_2	D_3	D_4	d_2
2	2.660	*	3.267	1.128	6	1.184	*	2.004	2.534
3	1.772	*	2.575	1.693	7	1.109	0.076	1.924	2.704
4	1.457	*	2.282	2.059	8	1.054	0.136	1.864	2.847
5	1.290	*	2.115	2.326	9	1.010	0.184	1.816	2.970
					10	0.975	0.223	1.777	3.078

*Lower control limits for R do not exist for sample sizes below 7.

Notes: Record all adjustments, tool changes, etc.

Subgroup No.	Date	Time	Comments

Control chart for attribute data

Part/Asm. Name	Operation		Nonconforming Units	Nonconformities:	Chart No
Part No.	Department		☐ np	☐ c	Average Sample Size
Parameter	Specification		☐ p	☐ u	Frequency

	1	2	3	4	5	6	7	8	9	10	11	12	13	14	15	16	17	18	19	20	21	22	23	24	25
Sample Size (n)																									
Number (np,c)																									
Proportion (p, u)																									
Date																									

Discrep-ancies

Notes: Record all adjustments, tool changes, etc.

Subgroup No.	Date	Time	Comments

Any change in people, materials, equipment, methods or environment should be noted. These notes will help you to take corrective or process improvement action when signaled by the control chart.

Continued on back

Control chart for attribute data calculation worksheet

	Nonconforming Units		**Nonconformities**

Number

(Subgroup sizes must be equal.)

np Chart

$$\text{UCL } np, \text{ LCL } np = n\bar{p} \pm 3 \sqrt{n\bar{p}\left(1 - \frac{n\bar{p}}{n}\right)}$$

c Chart

$$\text{UCL } c, \text{ LCL } c = \bar{c} \pm 3\sqrt{\bar{c}}$$

Proportion

(Subgroup sizes need not be equal.)

p Chart

$$\text{UCL } p, \text{ LCL } p = \bar{p} \pm 3 \sqrt{\frac{\bar{p}(1-\bar{p})}{n}}$$

u Chart

$$\text{UCL } u, \text{ LCL } u = \bar{u} \pm 3 \sqrt{\frac{\bar{u}}{n}}$$

$$\text{or} = \bar{p} \pm 3\frac{\sqrt{\bar{p}(1-\bar{p})}}{\sqrt{n}}$$

$$\text{or} = \bar{u} \pm 3\frac{\sqrt{\bar{u}}}{\sqrt{n}}$$

Notes: Record all adjustments, tool changes, etc.

Subgroup No.	Date	Time	Comments

Measurement system/gauge capability calculation worksheet

Part/Asm. Name	Gage Name	Part No.
Characteristic	Gage No.	Measurement Unit
Specification	Gage Type	Zero Equals

Operator	A				B				C			
Sample No.	1st Trial	2nd Trial	3rd Trial	Range	1st Trial	2nd Trial	3rd Trial	Range	1st Trial	2nd Trial	3rd Trial	Range
1												
2												
3												
4												
5												
6												
7												
8												
9												
10												
Totals												

$\bar{R}_A =$ 　　　　　 $\bar{R}_B =$ 　　　　　 $\bar{R}_C =$

Sum _____ Sum _____ Sum _____

$\bar{X}_A$ _____ $\bar{X}_B$ _____ $\bar{X}_C$ _____

Test for Control:

Upper Control Limit, $UCL_R = D_4 \bar{R} =$ _____ x _____ = _____

where: $\bar{R}$ is the average of: $\bar{R}_A + \bar{R}_B + \bar{R}_C =$ _____ + _____ + _____ = _____ = _____

$D_4 = 3.27$ for 2 trials or 2.58 for 3 trials.

If any individual range exceeds this limit, the measurement or reading should be reviewed, repeated, corrected or discarded as appropriate, and new averages and ranges should be computed.

Measurement System/Gage Capability Analysis:

Equipment Variation ("Repeatability") = $K_1 \bar{R} =$ _____ x _____ = _____ Repeatability

where: $K_1 = 4.56$ for 2 trials or 3.05 for 3 trials.

Operator Variation ("Reproducibility") = $K_2 \bar{X}_{diff} =$ _____ x _____ = _____ Reproducibility

where: $K_2 = 3.65$ for 2 operators or 2.70 for 3 operators.

$\bar{X}_{diff}$ is the difference between the $max_{\bar{x}}$ and $min_{\bar{x}}$.

Total "Repeatability" and "Reproducibility" Variation (R&R) = $\sqrt{(Repeatability)^2 + (Reproducibility)^2}$

$= \sqrt{(\text{\_\_\_\_\_})^2 + (\text{\_\_\_\_\_})^2} = \sqrt{\text{\_\_\_\_\_} + \text{\_\_\_\_\_}} = \sqrt{\text{\_\_\_\_\_}} =$ _____ Gage Capability

Gage Acceptability Determination:

$\dfrac{\text{Total Gage Capability (R\&R)}}{\text{Specification Tolerance}} =$ _____ = _____ %

Notes _____

_____

_____

_____

Analysis performed by: _____　　Date:

Constants and formulae for control charts

$\bar{X}$ and R, $\bar{X}$ and S charts

	$\bar{X}$ and R charts[a]				$\bar{X}$ and S charts[a]			
	Chart for averages ($\bar{X}$)	Chart for ranges (R)			Chart for averages ($\bar{X}$)	Chart for standard deviation(s)		
	Factors for control limits	Divisors for estimate of standard deviation	Factors for control limits		Factors for control limits	Divisors for estimate of standard deviation	Factors for control limits	
Sub-group size n	A_2	d_2	D_3	D_4	A_3	c_4	B_3	B_4
2	1.880	1.128	—	3.267	2.659	0.7979	—	3.267
3	1.023	1.693	—	2.574	1.954	0.8862	—	2.568
4	0.729	2.059	—	2.282	1.628	0.9213	—	2.266
5	0.577	2.326	—	2.114	1.427	0.9400	—	2.089
6	0.483	2.534	—	2.004	1.287	0.9515	0.030	1.970
7	0.419	2.704	0.076	1.924	1.182	0.9594	0.118	1.882
8	0.373	2.847	0.136	1.864	1.099	0.9650	0.185	1.815
9	0.337	2.970	0.184	1.816	1.032	0.9693	0.239	1.761
10	0.308	3.078	0.223	1.777	0.975	0.9727	0.284	1.716
11	0.285	3.173	0.256	1.744	0.927	0.9754	0.331	1.679
12	0.266	3.258	0.283	1.717	0.886	0.9776	0.354	1.646
13	0.249	3.336	0.307	1.693	0.850	0.9794	0.382	1.618
14	0.235	3.407	0.328	1.672	0.817	0.9810	0.406	1.594
15	0.223	3.472	0.347	1.653	0.789	0.9823	0.428	1.572
16	0.212	3.532	0.363	1.637	0.763	0.9835	0.448	1.552
17	0.203	3.588	0.378	1.622	0.739	0.9845	0.466	1.534
18	0.194	3.640	0.391	1.608	0.718	0.9854	0.482	1.518
19	0.187	3.689	0.403	1.597	0.698	0.9862	0.497	1.503
20	0.180	3.735	0.415	1.585	0.680	0.9869	0.510	1.490
21	0.173	3.778	0.425	1.575	0.633	0.9876	0.523	1.477
22	0.167	3.819	0.434	1.566	0.647	0.9882	0.534	1.466
23	0.162	3.858	0.443	1.557	0.633	0.9887	0.545	1.455
24	0.157	3.895	0.451	1.548	0.619	0.9892	0.555	1.445
25	0.153	3.931	0.459	1.541	0.606	0.9896	0.565	1.435

$$UCL_{\bar{x}}, LCL_{\bar{x}} = \bar{\bar{X}} \pm A_2\bar{R}$$
$$UCL_R = D_4\bar{R}$$
$$LCL_R = D_3R$$
$$\hat{\sigma} = \bar{R}/d_2$$

$$UCL_{\bar{x}}, LCL_{\bar{x}} = \bar{\bar{X}} \pm A_3\bar{s}$$
$$UCL_s = B_4\bar{s}$$
$$LCL_s = B_3\bar{s}$$
$$\hat{\sigma} = \bar{s}/c_4$$

[a] From ASTM publication STP-15D, *Manual on the Presentation of Data and Control Chart Analysis* (1976), pp 134–136.
© ASTM, 1916 Race Street, Philadelphia, Pennsylvania 19103. Reprinted with permission.

Median and individual charts

	Median charts[a, b]				Charts for individuals[a]			
	Chart for medians (X̃)	Chart for ranges (R)			Chart for individuals (X)	Chart for ranges (R)		
	Factors for control limits	Divisors for estimate of standard deviation	Factors for control limits		Factors for control limits	Divisors for estimate of standard deviation	Factors for control limits	
Subgroup size n	$\tilde{A}_2$	d_2	D_3	D_4	E_2	d_2	D_3	D_4
2	1.880	1.128	—	3.267	2.660	1.128	—	3.267
3	1.187	1.693	—	2.574	1.772	1.693	—	2.574
4	0.796	2.059	—	2.282	1.457	2.059	—	2.282
5	0.691	2.326	—	2.114	1.290	2.326	—	2.114
6	0.548	2.534	—	2.004	1.184	2.534	—	2.004
7	0.508	2.704	0.076	1.924	1.109	2.704	0.076	1.924
8	0.433	2.847	0.136	1.864	1.054	2.847	0.136	1.864
9	0.412	2.970	0.184	1.816	1.010	2.970	0.184	1.816
10	0.362	3.078	0.223	1.777	0.975	3,078	0.223	1.777

$$UCL_{\tilde{x}}, LCL_{\tilde{x}} = \tilde{X} \pm A_2\bar{R}$$
$$UCL_R = D_4\bar{R}$$
$$LCL_R = D_3R$$
$$\hat{\sigma} = \bar{R}/d_2$$

$$UCL_{\bar{x}}, LCL_{\bar{x}} = \bar{X} \pm E_2\bar{R}$$
$$UCL_R = D_4\bar{R}$$
$$LCL_R = D_3\bar{R}$$
$$\hat{\sigma} = \bar{R}/d_2$$

[a] From ASTM publication STP-15D, *Manual on the Presentation of Data and Control Chart Analysis* (1976), pp 134–136.
© ASTM, 1916 Race Street, Philadelphia, Pennsylvania 19103. Reprinted with permission.
[b] $\tilde{A}_2$ factors derived from ASTM STP-15D data and efficiency tables contained in W. J. Dixon and F. J. Massey, Jr. *Introduction to Statistical Analysis*, 3rd edn (1969), p. 488; McGraw-Hill Book Company, New York.

Example of X̄ and R chart construction

Steps	**Example**
1. Define purpose: quality characteristic	Response time
2. Collect data	X_1–X_4
3. Compute X̄ and R	5.25 1
4. Total X̄ and R	129.00 31

Day	X_1	X_2	X_3	X_4	Total	X̄	R̄
1	5	5	5	6	21	5.25	1
2	6	5	8	6	25	6.25	3
3	4	4	5	6	19	4.75	2
4	6	6	5	5	22	5.5	1
5	4	5	5	6	20	5.0	2
6	5	5	6	5	21	5.25	1
7	5	4	5	5	10	4.75	1
8	6	5	5	5	21	5.25	1
9	5	6	5	4	20	5.0	2
10	5	5	5	5	21	5.25	1
11	6	5	5	5	21	5.25	1
12	5	5	5	5	20	5.0	0
13	4	5	4	5	18	4.5	1
14	5	5	5	6	21	5.25	1
15	6	6	5	5	22	5.5	1
16	5	4	6	5	20	5.0	2
17	4	4	5	5	18	4.5	1
18	6	5	5	5	21	5.25	1
19	5	5	4	5	19	4.75	1
20	6	6	5	5	22	5.5	1
21	5	5	6	5	21	5.25	1
22	6	5	5	5	21	5.25	1
23	5	6	4	5	20	5.0	2
24	5	6	6	5	22	5.5	1
25	5	6	5	5	21	5.25	1
Totals						129.00	31

5. Compute average lines:

X̄ chart

$$\bar{\bar{X}} = \frac{129}{25} = 5.16$$

R chart

$$\bar{R} = \frac{31}{25} = 1.24$$

6. Compute control limits

- X̄ chart

$$UCL = \bar{\bar{X}} + A_2\bar{R} = 5.16 + (0.729 \times 1.24) = 6.06$$
$$LCL = \bar{\bar{X}} - A_2\bar{R} = 5.16 - (0.729 \times 1.24) = 4.26$$

- R chart

$$UCL = D_4\bar{R} = 2.282 \times 1.24 = 2.83$$
$$LCL = D_3\bar{R} = 0 \times 1.24 = 0$$

7. Construct chart

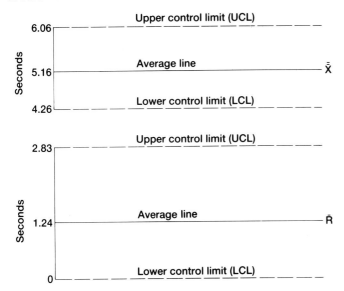

8. Plot points

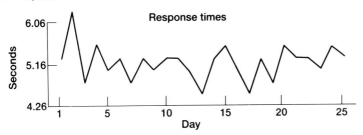

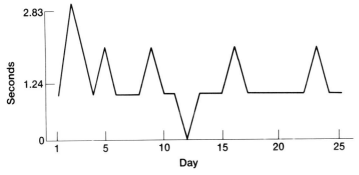

Recompute average
and control limits

**If process remains in
control, use last 25
points to recompute
average and control limits**

Individual measurements chart: pH readings of nickel baths

Sample	Reading	Range
1	3.2	
2	3.1	0.1
3	3.0	0.1
4	3.1	0.1
5	3.1	0
6	3.1	0
7	3.0	0.1
8	3.0	0
9	3.0	0
10	3.0	0
11	3.1	0.1
12	3.0	0.1
13	3.1	0.1
14	3.0	0.1
15	3.1	0.1
16	3.15	0.05
17	3.1	0.05
18	3.1	0
19	3.1	0
20	3.1	0
21	3.05	0.05
22	3.1	0.05
23	3.05	0.05
Totals	70.65	1.15

$$\bar{X} = \frac{70.65}{23} = 3.072 \qquad \bar{R} = \frac{1.15}{22} = 0.052$$

$$UCL = \bar{X} + \frac{3\bar{R}}{d_2} = 3.072 + \frac{3(0.052)}{1.128} = 3.21$$

$$LCL = \bar{X} - \frac{3\bar{R}}{d_2} = 3.072 - \frac{3(0.052)}{1.128} = 2.93$$

Formulae for hypothesis testing

Hypothesis	Test statistic and distribution
$H:\mu = \mu_0$ (the mean of a normal population is equal to a specified value μ_0; σ is known)	$Z = \dfrac{\bar{X} - \mu_0}{\sigma/\sqrt{n}}$ Normal distribution
$H:\mu = \mu_0$ (the mean of a normal population is equal to a specified value μ_0; σ is estimated by s)	$t = \dfrac{\bar{X} - \mu_0}{s/\sqrt{n}}$ t distribution with n − 1 degrees of freedom (d.f.)
$H:\mu_1 = \mu_2$ (the mean of population 1 is equal to the mean of population 2; assume that $\sigma_1 = \sigma_2$ and that both populations are normal)	$t = \dfrac{\bar{X}_1 - \bar{X}_2}{\sigma/\sqrt{1/n_1 + 1/n_2}\ \sqrt{[(n_1 - 1)s_1{}^2 + (n_2 - 1)s_2{}^2]/(n_1 + n_2 - 2)}}$ t distribution with d.f. $= n_1 + n_2 - 2$
$H:\sigma = \sigma_0$ (the standard deviation of a normal population is equal to a specified value σ_0)	$\chi^2 = \dfrac{(n - 1)s^2}{\sigma_0{}^2}$ Chi-square distribution with d.f. $= n - 1$
$H:\sigma_1 = \sigma_2$ (the standard deviation of population 1 is equal to the standard deviation of population 2; assume that both populations are normal)	$F = \dfrac{s_1^2}{s_2^2}$ F distribution with d.f.$_1 = n_1 - 1$ and d.f.$_2 = n_2 - 1$
$H:p = p_0$ (the fraction defective in a population is equal to a specified value p_0; assume that $np_0 \geqslant 5$)	$Z = \dfrac{p - p_0}{\sqrt{p_0(1 - p_0)/n}}$ Normal distribution
$H:p_1 = p_2$ (the fraction defective in population 1 is equal to the fraction defective in population 2; assume that n_1p_1 and n_2p_2 are each $\geqslant 5$)	$Z = \dfrac{X_1/n_1 - X_2/n_2}{\sqrt{\hat{p}(1 - \hat{p})(1/n_1 + 1/n_2)}}$ $\hat{p} = \dfrac{X_1 + X_2}{n_1 + n_2}$ Normal distribution

Confidence limits formulae

Parameters	Formulae
Mean of a normal population (standard deviation known)	$\bar{X} \pm Z_{\alpha/2} \dfrac{\sigma}{\sqrt{n}}$

where $\bar{X}$ = sample average
Z = normal distribution coefficient
σ = standard deviation of population
n = sample size

Mean of a normal population (standard deviation unknown)	$\bar{X} \pm t_{\alpha/2} \dfrac{s}{\sqrt{n}}$

where t = distribution coefficient (with $n-1$ degrees of freedom)
s = estimated σ

Standard deviation of a normal population	Upper confidence limit = $s\sqrt{\dfrac{n-1}{\chi^2_{\alpha/2}}}$
	Lower confidence limit = $s\sqrt{\dfrac{n-1}{\chi^2_{1-\alpha/2}}}$

where χ^2 = chi-square distribution coefficient with $n-1$ degrees of freedom
$1-\alpha$ = confidence level

Difference between the means of two normal populations (standard deviations $\sigma_1 = \sigma_2$ known)	$(\bar{X}_1 - \bar{X}_2) \pm Z_{\alpha/2} \sqrt{\dfrac{\sigma_1^2}{n_1} + \dfrac{\sigma_2^2}{n_2}}$

Difference between the means of two normal populations ($\sigma_1 = \sigma_2$ but unknown)	$(\bar{X}_1 - \bar{X}_2) \pm t_{\alpha/2} \sqrt{\dfrac{1}{n_1} + \dfrac{1}{n_2}}$
	$\times \sqrt{\dfrac{\sum (X - X_1)^2 + \sum (X - X_2)^2}{n_1 + n_2 - 2}}$

Mean time between failures based on an exponential population of time between failures	Upper confidence limit = $\dfrac{2rm}{\chi^2_{\alpha/2}}$
	Lower confidence limit = $\dfrac{2rm}{\chi^2_{1-\alpha/2}}$

where r = number of occurences in the sample (i.e., number of failures)
m = sample mean time between failures
$DF = 2r$

Instruments for assessing cost of quality

Task anaylsis for cost of quality

TASK NAME:	
GENERAL DESCRIPTION OF WORK ELEMENTS WITHIN THIS TASK	
ELEMENT CODE	DESCRIPTION
ANALYST NAME:	DEPARTMENT: DATE:
MANAGER'S APPROVAL:	DATE:

Task anaylsis for cost of quality

TASK NAME:

What are your customer requirements for this task?

Are you and your customer in agreement on these requirements?
(   )   YES   (   )   NO

What problems do poor quality outputs create?

How can/do you measure the quality of the outputs you deliver?

What are the input requirements needed to perform this task?

Are you and your suppliers in agreement on requirements?
(   )   YES   (   )   NO

What problems do poor quality inputs create?

How can/do you measure the quality of the inputs you receive?

ANALYST NAME: DEPARTMENT: DATE:

MANAGER'S APPROVAL: DATE:

Task anaylsis for cost of quality

IMPROVEMENT PRIORITY #	TASK	APP	PREV	FAIL	NON COQ

ANALYST NAME:	DEPARTMENT:	DATE:
MANAGER'S APPROVAL:	DATE:	

Task anaylsis for cost of quality

TASK NAME:

How do you monitor and measure the quality of your value add on this task?

How do you cause poor quality on this task?

What should be done for improvement?

How can improvement be measured?

How many hours/week are spent on this task?   _____hrs/wk

These hours are either a cost of doing business, a cost of quality, or some combination of the two.
How do you classify them?

| | Business | _____hrs/wk |
| Cost of Quality = (COQ) = | | _____hrs/wk |

COQ hours can be further classified as appraisal, prevention, and failure. What are they?

	Appraisal	_____hrs/wk
	Prevention	_____hrs/wk
	Failure	_____hrs/wk
	TOTAL COQ	_____hrs/wk

ANALYST NAME: DEPARTMENT: DATE:

MANAGER'S APPROVAL: DATE:

Task anaylsis for cost of quality

TASK NAME:	
TASK INPUT:	_____
	_____
INPUT SOURCE:	_____
	_____
TASK OUTPUT:	_____
	_____
	_____
OUTPUT TO:	_____
	_____
QUESTION VALUE ADD OF EVERY ELEMENT IN INPUT-OUTPUT KEY AREAS OF EMPHASIS:	_____
	_____
	_____
	_____
	_____
	_____
ANALYST NAME:	DEPARTMENT: DATE:
MANAGER'S APPROVAL:	DATE:

Change and effect

THEME	PROBLEM EVALUATION							
	TOTAL VALUE	CHANGE DIFFICULTY			EFFECT BENEFITS			
PROBLEM I.D.	C+E	1 CANT	2 HARD	3 EASY	1 NONE	2 SMAL	3 LARG	

Equalisation factor for productivity and quality assessment using productivity and quality task responsibility curve (PQTRC)

The equalisation factor (E_f) is recommended as a measure of balance at the individual and group levels.

$$E_f = 0.0167\, N_{it} \sum_{i=1}^{n} T_{it}$$

where:
E_f = equalisation factor representing a measure of balance between individuals and work groups whose processing time for a specific task, i, in period, t, is known.
T_{it} = Time to complete a specific task, i, by an individual or work group in period t.
N_{it} = Number of items completed by unit time for task, i, in period, t.
n = Number of workstations involved in completing task, i, in period, t.

Learning curve formulae using productivity and quality task responsibility curve (PQTRC)

When trying to examine the learning effect involved in moving performance between two points on the productivity and quality task responsibility curve (PQTRC). The following formulae are suggested.

- **Formula 1**
  Learning factor (K) can be calculated

$$K = \frac{\log t1 - \log ta}{\log n}$$

- **Formula 2**
  The final time required to complete the task nth time can be determined

$$t_n = t_1 \left(\frac{1 - K}{n^k} \right)$$

- **Formula 3**
  The improvement ratio which helps determine how many times a task must be completed before improvement flattens can be determined

$$n \geq \frac{1}{1 - R_t^{1/k}}$$

- **Formula 4**
  The average time (t_a) declines according to:

$$t_a = \frac{t}{n^K}$$

As the individual or work group gains experience, each succeeding unit is produced in less time.

Where K, learning factor; R_t ratio of time to perform the task for the nth time divided by time to perform for the $(n - 1)$th time; t_1, time to complete the task the first time; t_a, total average unit time after completing the task n times; I, time improvement factor; n, number of times the task has been completed; t_n, time to perform the task nth time; I_n, total time to perform the task n times.

● **Equation 5**

Reasonable goal for improvement in unit time can be calculated by:

$$n_2 = \frac{n_1}{I^{1/K}}$$

Correlation coefficient formulae using productivity and quality assessment matrix (PAQAM)

The rank correlation coefficient and sample correlation coefficient that can be used to compare P_i and Q_i paired data, using productivity and quality assessment matrix (PAQAM) and the productivity and quality task responsibility curve (PQTRC), can be calculated as follows:

Let:

TO_{it} = Total output of task, i, in period, t.

TI_{it} = Total input utilised to produce output of task, i, in period, t.

TP_{it} = Total productivity of task, i, in period, t.

QI_{it} = Quality index of task, i, in period, t.

(P_i, Q_i) = Paired productivity and quality data for each individual performing task i, in period, t. $(i = 1, 2, \ldots, n)$.

D_i^2 = The difference between the ranks assigned to P_i and Q_i.

SCC_{it} = Sample correlation coefficient for paired data (P_i, Q_i) assuming bivariate normal population.

RCC_{it} = The rank correlation coefficient that can be used to compare P_i and Q using PAQAM and PQTRC.

ML = Maximum likelihood function that can be used to obtain the mean variance and CC_{it} of (P_i, Q_i) paired data by differentiation method.

$$ML = \overset{n}{\underset{i=1}{\pi}} \, f\,(P_i, Q_i)$$

Therefore, by definition

$$TP_{it} = \frac{TO_{it}}{TI_{it}}$$

$$RCC_{it} = 1 - \frac{6 \cdot \sum\limits_{i=1}^{n} D_i^2}{n(n^2 - 1)}$$

$$SCC_{it} = \frac{n \cdot \sum\limits_{i=1}^{n} P_i Q_i - \left(\sum\limits_{i=1}^{n} P_i\right)\left(\sum\limits_{i=1}^{n} Q_i\right)}{\sqrt{n \cdot \sum\limits_{i=1}^{n} P_i^2 - \left(\sum\limits_{i=1}^{n} P_i\right)^2} \sqrt{n \cdot \sum\limits_{i=1}^{n} Q_i^2 - \left(\sum\limits_{i=1}^{n_1} Q_i\right)^2}}$$

BIBLIOGRAPHY

Adam, E. E. Jr., Hershauer, J. C. and Ruch, W. A. (1978). Measuring the Quality Dimension of Service Productivity. National Science Foundation, U.S. Department of Commerce, Washington, D.C.

Adam, E. E. Jr., Hershauer, J. C. and Ruch, W. A. 1981. Productivity and Quality: Measurement as a Basis for Improvement. Prentice-Hall, Englewood Cliffs, New Jersey.

Adam, N. R. and Dogramaci, A. (Eds.) (1981). Productivity Analysis at Organizational Level. Kluwer Boston, Hingham, Massachusetts.

Aggarwal, S. C. (1979). A study of productivity measures for improving benefit cost ratios of operating organization. Proceedings 5th International Conference Production Research, Amsterdam, The Netherlands, August 12–16, pp. 64–70.

American National Standards Institute (1975). Guide for Quality Control and Control Chart Method of Analyzing Data. ASQC Standards B1-1958 and B2-1958/ANSI Z1. 1958 and Z1.2-1958, revised.

American National Standards Institute (1975). Control Chart Method of Controlling Quality During Production. ASQC Standard B3-1958/ANSI Z1.3-1958, revised.

American Society for Quality Control (1971). "Quality Costs – What and How." ASQC, Milwaukee, WI.

American Society for Quality Control (1976). QC Circles: Applications, Tools, and Theory. ASQC, 161 West Wisconsin Avenue 53203.

American Society for Testing Materials (1951). ASTM Manual on Quality Control of Materials. ASTM, Philadelphia.

American Society for Testing and Materials (1976). ASTM Manual on Presentation of Data and Control Chart Analysis. ASTM, Philadelphia.

Amsden, R. T., Butler, H. E. and Amsdem, D. M. (1986). SPC Simplified: Practical Steps to Quality. UNIPUB, White Plains, New York.

Arrow, K. J., Chenery, H. B., Minhas, B. S. and Solow, R. M. (1961). Capital-labor substitution and economic efficiency. *Rev. Econ. Stat.,* 18, 225–250.

Bemesderfer, J. L. (1979). Approving a process for production. *Journal of Quality Technology,* January, 1–12.

Berger, W. (1978). Micro computers and software quality control. ASQC Annual Technical Conference Transactions, p. 328.

Bernolak, I. (1976). Enhancement of productivity through inter-firm comparisons, a Canadian experience. In: Improving Productivity Through Industry and Company Measurement, Series 2, pp. 59–65. National Center for Productivity and Quality of Working Life, U.S. Govt. Printing Office, Washington, D.C.

Besterfield, D. H. (1979). Quality Control. Prentice-Hall, Englewood Cliffs, N. J.

Blank, Lee and Solorzano, Jorge (1978). Using Quality Cost Analysis for Management Improvement. *Industrial Engineering 10,* 46–51.

Bowen, W. (1979). Better prospects for our ailing productivity. *Fortune,* December 3, 68–76.

Box, G. E. P., Hunter, W. G. and Hunter, S. J. (1978). Statistics for Experimenters. John Wiley and Sons, New York.

Bradley, J. W. and Korn, D. H. Acquisition and Corporate Development: A Contemporary Perspective for the Manager. Arthur D. Little, Lexington, Massachusetts.

Brewer, C. C. (1980). Innovations in Quality Cost in the New Decade. *American Society of Quality Control 34th Annual Technical Conference Transactions.* ASQC, Atlanta, GA.

Bross, I. D. (1953). Design for Decision. Macmillan, New York.

Brown, F. X. (1980). Quality Costs and Strategic Planning. *American Society for Quality Control 34th Annual Technical Conference Transactions.* ASQC, Atlanta, GA.

Buehler, V. M. and Shetty, Y. K. (1981). Productivity Improvement. Case Studies of Proven Practice. AMACOM, New York.

Burr, I. W. (1979). Elementary Statistical Quality Control. Marcel Dekker, New York.

Calvin, T. W. (1983). Quality Control Techniques for "Zero Defects". *IEEE Transactions on Components, Hybrids and Manufacturing Technology CHMT-6,* 3, 323–328.

Campbell, D. T. and Stanley, J. C. (1963). Experimental and Quasi Experimental Design for Research. Rand McNally, Chicago.

Caplan, F. (1985). Managing for Success Through the Quality System. *Quality Progress 18,* 29–32, 57–58.

Carter, C. W. and Olson, R. C. (1980). Rating Quality Systems. *Quality Progress 13,* 20–22.

Charbonneau, H. C., and Webster, G. L. (1978). Industrial Quality Control. Prentice-Hall, Englewood Cliffs, New Jersey.

Cheng, Philip C. (1976). A Conceptual Analysis of Quality Control Cost for Industrial Management Decision Making. *Industrial Management 18,* 28–31.

Clark, John. (1985). Costing for Quality at Celanese. *Management Accounting 66,* 42–46.

Cleverley, D. S. (1983). Product Quality Level Monitoring and Control for Logic Chips and Modules. *IBM Journal of Research and Development 27,* 4–10.

Cohen, C. D. (1981). Statistical Sampling for Bank Auditors. Bank Administration Institute, Park Ridge Ill.

Cole, R. E. (1980). Learning from the Japanese: Prospects and Pitfalls. *Management Review.* September.

Cole, R. E. (1981). The Japanese lesson in quality. *Technology Review,* July, 29.

Craig, C. E. and Harris, C. R. (1972). Productivity concepts and measurement – a management viewpoint. Unpublished Master's Thesis. MIT, Cambridge, Massachusetts.

Craig, C. E. and Harris, C. R. (1973). Total productivity measurement at the firm level. *Sloan Management Review,* 21, 37–46.

Crandall, N. F. and Wooton, L. M. (1978). Development strategies of organizational productivity, *California Management Review*, 21, 37-46.

Crosby, P. B. (1979). Quality is Free. McGraw-Hill, New York.

Danforth, D. D. (1984). Quality means doing the job right the first time. *The Wall Street Journal*, March 21, 33.

Davies, O. L. (1954). Design and Analysis of Industrial Experiments. Oliver and Boyd, London.

Deming, W. E. (1982). Quality, Productivity and Competitive Position. MIT Press, Cambridge, Mass.

Deming, W. E. (1986). Out of the Crisis. MIT Press, Cambridge, Mass.

Dewar, D. L. (1980). The Quality Circle Handbook. Quality Circle Institute, Red Bluff, California.

Dewitt, F. (1970). Technique for measuring management productivity. *Management Review*, 59, 2–11.

Dewitt, F. (1976). Productivity and the industrial engineer. *Industrial Engineering*, 8, 20–27.

Diamond, W. J. Practical Experiment Designs for Engineers and Scientists. Lifetime Learning Publications, Division of Wadsworth, Inc., Belmont, California.

Dickinson, Michael J. (1984). How Quality Caused a Turnaround. *Quality 23*, 16–19.

Domar, E. D. *et al.* (1964). Economic growth and productivity in the United States, Canada, United Kingdom, Germany and Japan in the post-war period. *Rev. Econ. Stat.*, 46, 33–40.

Doyle, M. and Straus, D. (1978). How to Make Meetings Work. Playboy Paperbacks, New York.

Duncan, A. J. (1974). Quality Control and Industrial Statistics, Richard D. Irwin, Inc., Homewood, Ill.

Ebrahimpour, Mailing (1985). An Examination of Quality Management in Japan: Implications for Management in the United States. *Journal of Operations Management* 5, 419–431.

Edosomwan, Johnson A. Just-in-time Total Productivity and Quality Management. Working Paper, IBM Technical Publications.

Edosomwan, Johnson A. The Effect to Technology on the Relationship Between Productivity and Quality. Working Paper, *International Journal of Technology Management*.

Edosomwan, Johnson A. (1958). A task-oriented total productivity measurement model for electronic printed circuit board assembly. International Electronic Assembly Conference Proceedings, October 7–9, Santa Clara, California.

Edosomwan, Johnson A. (1980). Implementation of the total productivity model in a manufacturing company. Master's Thesis, Department of Industrial Engineering, University of Miami, July.

Edosomwan, Johnson A. (1983). Production and service improvement technique (PASIT). Unpublished manual. IBM Data Systems Division, New York.

Edosomwan, Johnson A. (1983). Quality error removal technique. Unpublished Manual, IBM Data Systems Division, New York.

Edosomwan, Johnson A. (1985). A methodology for assessing the impact of computer technology on productivity, production quality, job satisfaction and psychological stress in a specific assembly task. Doctoral Dissertation, Department of Engineering Administration, The George Washington University, Washington, D.C. 20052, January. Grant SS-36-83-21, Social Science Research Council (U.S. Department of Labor) and IBM 2J2/2K5/-722271/83/85.

Edosomwan, Johnson A. (1986). Robotics-aided task impact model for the new frontier in manufacturing. Proceedings of Second World Conference on robotics research. Robotic Research transactions published by Society of Manufacturing Engineers (SME).

Edosomwan, Johnson A. (1986). A conceptual framework for productivity planning. *Industrial Engineering*, January.

Edosomwan, Johnson A. (1986). Managing technology in the workplace: A challenge for industrial engineers. *Industrial Engineering*, February, pp. 14–18.

Edosomwan, Johnson A. (1986). The impact of computer-aided manufacturing on total productivity. Proceedings for the 8th Annual Conference on Computers and Industrial Engineering, Orlando, Florida, March.

Edosomwan, Johnson A. (1986). A methodology for assessing the impact of robotics on total productivity in an assembly task. Proceedings of Annual International Industrial Engineering Conference, May, Dallas, Texas.

Edosomwan, Johnson, A. (1986). Statistical process control in group technology production environment. SYNERGY '86 Proceedings, June 16–18, Universal City, California. Sponsored by Society of Manufacturing Engineers, Computer and Automated Systems Association, and the American Production and Inventory Control Society.

Edosomwan, Johnson A. (1986). Technology impact on the quality of working life – challenge for engineering managers in the year 2000. Proceedings of the First International Conference on Engineering Management, September, Washington, D.C.

Edosomwan, Johnson A. (1986). Productivity management in computer aided manufacturing environment. Proceedings of the First International Conference on Engineering Management, September, Washington, D.C.

Edosomwan, Johnson A. (1986). Productivity Management in Computer-aided Manufacturing Environment. Proceedings for the First International Conference on Engineering Management, Arlington, Virginia, September.

Edosomwan, Johnson A. (1986). Productivity and Quality Management – A Challenge in the Year 2000. Proceedings for the Annual International Industrial Engineering Conference, Boston, Mass., December.

Edosomwan, Johnson A. (1986). Statistical Process Control in Electronics Printed Circuit Board Assembly. Proceedings for the Annual Fall Industrial Engineering Conference, Boston, Mass., December.

Edosomwan, Johnson A. (1987). Integrating Productivity and Quality Management. Marcel Dekker, Inc., New York.

Edosomwan, Johnson A. (1987). Managing Productivity and Quality in a Production Environment. Proceedings for the IBM Symposium on Quality and Reliability, July.

Edosomwan, Johnson A. (1987). The Challenge for Industrial Managers: Productivity and Quality in the Work Place. *Industrial Management*, September/October.

Edosomwan, Johnson A. (1987). Understanding the Connection Between Productivity and Quality in a Competitive Business Environment. Keynote address presented in the Proceedings for the IFS Conference on SPC, Birmingham, England, November.

Edosomwan, Johnson A. (1988). A Program for Managing Service Quality. Working Paper for Service Quality. (Ed. Spechler, J.). IE and Management Press.

Edosomwan, Johnson A. (1989). A Framework for Balancing Productivity and Quality Requirements. Working Paper for the Second International Conference on Productivity Research, Miami, Florida, February.

Edosomwan, Johnson A. and Sumanth, D. J. (1988). A Practical Guide for Productivity Measurement in Organizations. Working Manual. UNIPUB, New York.

Elder, John P., Sundstorm, Brezinski, William, Waldeck, John P., Calpin, James P. and Boggs, Stephen A. An Organizational Behavior Management Approach to Quality Assurance in a Community Health Mental Center. *Journal of Organizational Behavior Management 5*, nos.3,4 12 (Fall/Winter 1983): 19–35.

Enrick, N. L. (1977). Quality Control and Reliability. Industrial Press, New York.

Ewing, D. W. (Ed.) (1964). Long-Range Planning for Management. Harper and Row, New York.

Fabricant, S. (1962). Which Productivity? Perspective on a current question. *Monthly Labor Review*, 86, 609–613.

Fabricant, S. (1969). A Primer on Productivity. Random House, New York.

Feigenbaum, A. V. (1979). American manufactures strive for quality – Japanese style. *Business Week*, March 12, p. 5.

Feigenbaum, A. V. (1983). *Total Quality Control*. McGraw-Hill, New York.

Feigenbaum, A. V. (1984) The Hard Road to Quality Excellence. *National Productivity Review 3*, 442–445.

Feigenbaum, A. V., Midas, Michael Jr. and Clark, R. H. (1982). Quality – A Productivity Plan. *Quality 21*, no. 8 (August 1982), Q1–Q14.

Feilden, G. B. R. (1978). The Role of Standards in Quality Assurance. *Quality Assurance 4*, 71–82.

Fein, M. (1974). Rational Approaches to Raising Productivity. Monograph Series No. 5, American Institute of Industrial Engineering, Norcross, Georgia.

Fetter, R. B. (1967). The Quality Control System. Richard D. Irwin, Homewood, Illinois.

Flohr, John R. (1974). In Total Quality Assurance, Training is Vital. *Management Review 63*, 25–31.

Forys, J. R. (1986). Redefining Quality Awareness. *Quality Progress 19*, 14–17.

Frazer, V. C. M. and Dale, B. G. (1986). U.K. Quality Circle Failures – The Latest Picture. *Omega 14*, 23–33.

Freund, R. A. and Trulli, H. B. (1982). Quality Assurance Review Techniques. *Journal of Quality Technology 14*, 122–129.

Friesecke, Raymond F. (1983). The Quality Revolution; A Challenge to Management. *Managerial Planning 32*, 7–9, 26.

Geare, A. J. (1976). Productivity from Scanlon-type plans. *Academic Management Review*, 99–107.

Gold, B. (1976). Tracing gaps between expectations and results of technological innovation: The case of iron and steel. *Journal of Industrial Economics*, September.

Goldstein, R. (1980). Quality Modeling With Dissipative Networks. *American Society of Quality Control 34th Annual Technical Conference Transactions* (May 20–22, 1980): Atlanta, GA.

Goodwin, E. W. Quality is Free. *MTM Journal of Methods – Time Measurement, 11* 14–19.

Goodwin, H. F. (1968). Improvements must be managed. *Journal of Industrial Engineering*, No. 11, 538–543.

Grant, E. L. and Leavenworth, R. S. (1980). *Statistical Quality Control*. 5th Ed., McGraw-Hill, New York.

Hassan, M. Zia and Knowles, T. W. (1979). An Optimal Quality Control Design for a Single Product Serial Manufacturing System. *Journal of Quality Technology, 11*, 20–27.

Hassan, M. Zia and Manaspiti, Aphai (1982). Quality Control Design for a Single Product Manufacturing System Subject to Inspection Error. *Engineering Costs & Production Economics*, April, 99–117.

Hayes, Glen E. and Romig, Harry G. (1977). Modern Quality Control. Bruce.

Hoadley, B. (1981). The Quality Measurement Plan (QMP). *Bell System Technical Journal, 60*, 215–273.

Hotard, Daniel G. and Jordan, Joe D. (1981). Regression Analysis is Applied to Improve Product Quality. *Industrial Engineering, 13*, 68, 70–75.

Huff, D. (1954). How to Lie with Statistics. Norton, New York.

IBM Data Systems Division. Teaming up for Quality: Quality Excellence Teams Education Guide. Poughkeepsie, New York 12602.

IBM Quality Institute (1985). Process Control, Capability and Improvement. The Quality Institute, Southbury, Connecticut.

Irving, Robert R. (1983). Quality Control by the Numbers. *Iron Age 226*, 37–44.

Ishikawa, K. (1976). Guide to Quality Control. Asian Productivity Organization, Tokyo.

Ishikawa, K. (1985). What is Total Quality Control? – The Japanese Way. Translated by David J. Lu. Prentice Hall, New York.

Jamieson, A. (1982). Introduction to Quality Control. Reston Publishing Co., Reston, VA.

Japan: Quality Control and Innovation. (Special Advertising Section) *Business Week* (July 20, 1981): 18–44.

Juran, J. M. (1964). Managerial Breakthrough. McGraw-Hill, New York.

Juran, J. M. (1978). Life Behind the Quality Dikes. European Organization for Quality Control, 22nd Annual Conference, Dresden.

Juran, J. M. (1979). Quality Control Handbook. McGraw-Hill, New York.

Juran, J. N. (1981). Product Quality – A Presentation for the West. Management Review, American Management Association, June/July, p. 16.

Juran, J. M., Gryna, F. M. Jr., and Bingham, R. S. Jr. (1979). Quality Control Handbook, 3rd Ed. McGraw-Hill, New York.

Kackar, R. N. (1985). Off-Line Quality Control, Parameter Design, and the Taguchi Method. *Journal of Quality Technology 17*, 176–188.

Kapur, R. and Liles, D. H. (1982). Job Design for Persons with Physical Disabilities. pp. 169–178. AIIE Proceedings Annual Spring Conf., May.

Kaufman, Roger (1976). Identifying and Solving Problems: a System Approach. University Associates, Inc., La Jolla, CA.

Kendrick, J. W., in Collaboration with the American Productivity Center (1984). Improving Company Productivity. Handbook with Case Studies. The Johns Hopkins University Press, Baltimore.

Kendrick, J. W. and Creamer, D. (1965). Measuring Company Productivity: Handbook with Case Studies (Studies in Business Economics, No. 89). National Industrial Conference Board, New York.

Konz, S. (1979). Quality Circles: Japan Success Story. *Industrial Engineering,* 11, 24–28.

Ott, Ellis R. (1975). Process Quality Control. McGraw-Hill Book Company, New York.

Product Quality: How to get It; How to Keep it. (1954). *Chief Executive* 19, 20–33.

Putnam, Arnold O. (1983). Three Quality Issues American Management Still Avoids. *Quality Progress 16*, No. 12, 12–25.

Quality Costs: "Costs of Quality" and "Quality Costs" – The Difference. (1985) *Small Business Report 10*, No. 11 85–88.

Quality and Productivity (1977). *Quality Progress 10*, No. 11, 18–21.

Rae, J. C. (1979). Establishing a Cost Effective System of Total Quality. *Quality Assurance 5*, 85–88.

Reddy, Jack A. (1983). Three Essentials of Product Quality. *Harvard Business Review 83*, 153–159.

Schilling, E. G. (1982). Acceptance Sampling in Quality Control. Marcel Decker, New York.

Schonberger, Richard J. (1984). Just-In-Time Production – The Quality Dividend. *Quality Progress 17*, No. 10, 22–24.

Schrock E. M. (1977). How to Manufacture a Quality Product. *Quality Progress 10*, No. 8, 25–27.

Shewhart, W. A. (1931). Economic Control of Quality of Manufactured Product. Van Nostrand, New York.

Sinha, Madhav N. and Wilborn, Walter W. O. (1983). Auditing for Quality Control. *Internal Auditor 40*, No. 5, 18–21.

Sink, D. S. (1985). Productivity Management: Planning, Measurement, Evaluation and Control. John Wiley, New York.

Stiles, E. M. (1981). Handbook for Total Quality Assurance. Bureau of Business Practice, Conn.

Sullivan, L. P. (1984). Reducing Variability: A New Approach to Quality. *Quality Progress 17*, No. 7, 15–21.

Sumanth, D. J. (1984). Productivity Engineering and Management. McGraw-Hill Book Company, New York.

Toellner, J. (1981). Building Management Acceptance of Quality Assurance. *Infosystems 28*, No. 5, 100–102.

Tsuda-Yoshikazu and Tribus, Myron (1985). Managing for Quality: Does Culture Make a Difference? *Quality Progress 18*, No. 11, 23–29.

Weatherston, David (1985). The Mark of Quality Management. *Industrial Management 9*, No. 10, 21–23.

U.S. Department of Commerce, National Bureau of Standards. (1969). Precision Measurement and Calibration: Statistical Concepts and Procedures. U.S. Government Printing Office, Washington, D.C.

Warnecke, H.-J., Bullinger, H.-J. and Kolle, J. H. (1981). German Manufacturing Industry Approaches to Increasing Flexibility and Productivity. AIIE Proceedings Annual Spring Conference, pp. 643–651, May.

Weimer, George A. (1985). SPC Now a Must to Gain Quality. *Iron Age 22*, No. 8 (April 19), 51–59.

Welkowitz, J., Ewen, R. B., and Cohen, J. (1971). Introductory Statistics for the Behavioral Sciences. Academic Press, New York.

Western Electric Co. (1956). Statistical Quality Control Handbook. Available from I.D.C. Commercial Sales, Western Electric Company, P.O. Box 26205, Indianapolis, Indiana 46226.

Wilson, M. F. (1967). The Quality Your Customer Sees. *Journal of the Electronics Division ASQC*, July, pp. 4–16.

Wolff, Michael F. (1986). Quality/Process Control: What R&D Can Do. *Research Management 29*, No.1 (January/February 1986): 9–11.

Zubairi, M. Mazhar (1985). Statistical Process Control Management Issues. 1985 Proceedings for the Annual International Industrial Engineering Conference.

GLOSSARY: Common terms in productivity and quality management

accuracy   Deviation of the measured or observed value from the true value (see also *precision*).

advanced statistical methods   More sophisticated and less widely applicable techniques of statistical process analysis and control than included in basic statistical methods; this can include more advanced control chart techniques, regression analysis, design of experiments, and advanced problem-solving techniques.

allocation criteria   Used for allocating overhead expenses to the various input and output components.

arithmetic means   Often referred to as the average of the population.

assignable causes or **special causes**   Causes that the operator can do something about; detectable because they are not always active in the process. We can see assignable causes because they have a stronger effect on the process than chance causes.

attribute chart   A type of chart in which characteristics are not measured in numbers but are considered acceptable or not acceptable, good or bad. The p-chart is an example of an attribute chart.

attributes data   Quantitative data that can be counted for recording and analysis.

attributes   Non-measurable characteristics. They are either present or they are not.

average   The result of dividing the total or sum of a group of measurements by the number of things measured. Average is another term for 'mean'.

average and range chart   The most commonly used variable chart, also called $\bar{X}$–R (X bar R) chart.

average range $(\bar{R})$ The mean or the average value of a group of ranges on an average and range chart. It is used to calculate control limits for both averages and ranges on the average and range chart.

awareness   Personal understanding of the interrelationship of quality and productivity, directing attention to the requirement for management commitment and statistical thinking to achieve never-ending improvement.

basic statistical methods   These apply the theory of variation through the use of basic problem-solving techniques and statistical process control; they include control chart construction and interpretation (for both variables and attributes data) and capability analysis.

binomial distribution   Discrete probability distribution for attributes data that applies to conforming and nonconforming units and underlies the p and np charts.

block   Part of the experimental material that is likely to be more homogeneous than the whole.

boundaries   A line between one interval and the next in the frequency histogram.

brainstorming   A group problem-solving method to bring out many ideas in a short time.

c-chart   A type of attribute control chart that helps monitor the number or count of defects part by part, or by inspection units, in a production run.

capability   When the process average, plus and minus, and 3σ spread of the distribution of individuals $(\bar{X} + 3\sigma)$ is contained within the specification tolerance (variables data), or when at least 99.73% of individuals are within specification (attributes data), a process is said to be capable. Efforts to improve capability must continue, however, consistent with the operational philosophy of never-ending improvement in quality and productivity. Capability can be determined only after the process is in statistical control.

capability index   The number that expresses the capability of a process or machine. (See *machine capability* and *process capability*.) To find this index number, compare the process spread to the specification spread and express it in terms of the standard deviation. The C_p index does not take into account where the process is centred with respect to the tolerance of the part.

capability ratio   The ratio of the machine or process spread (6σ) to the specification tolerance, expressed as a percentage.

capital   The investment in natural resources, reproducible capital (structures, machinery, equipment, and inventories), and financial assets, excluding investments in government debt and in securities of other enterprises.

capital compensation   Income accruing to owners of property in the form of interest, rent, royalties, and profits.

capital consumption   Using up stored services and the resulting decline in value of reproducible durable capital as a result of ageing, deterioration, and obsolescence; not to be confused with capital input, which represents the use of extant capital goods.

capital, fixed   Sum of the value of land, structures, machinery, and equipment.

capital, working   Sum of the value of cash, accounts and notes receivable and inventories.

cause and effect diagram   A diagram that shows in picture or graph form how causes relate to the stated effect or to one another. Also known as a fishbone diagram.

central line   The line on a control chart that represents the average or median value of the items being plotted.

characteristic A distinguishing feature of a process or its output on which variables or attributes data can be collected.

chronic problem A type of problem that happens over and over again.

common cause A source of variation that affects all the individual values of the process output being studied; in control chart analysis it appears as part of the random process variation.

comparative experiment An experiment whose objective is to compare the treatments rather than to determine absolute values.

comprehensive quality planning The process of assessing all factors that may affect product or service quality throughout the specified life cycle.

continuous improvement in quality and productivity The operational philosophy that makes best use of the talents within the company to produce products of increasing quality in an increasingly efficient way that protects the return of investment.

control chart A graphical representation of a characteristic of a process, showing plotted value of some statistic gathered from that characteristic, a central line, and one or two control limits; minimises the net economic loss from type I and type II errors; has two basic uses: as a judgment to determine if a process has been operating in statistical control, and as an operation to aid in maintaining statistical control.

control limits A line (or lines) on a control chart used as a basis for judging the significance of the variation from subgroup to subgroup; variation beyond a control limit is evidence that special causes are affecting the process; control limits are calculated from process data and are not to be confused with engineering specifications.

deflation (price) Dividing an economic time series expressed in value terms by an index of prices of the underlying physical units (combined by appropriate quantity weights) in order to convert the series to 'real' terms or constant prices.

deflator Generally an index of price used to bring the current monetary output and/or input(s) to base-period terms; a deflator can be less than 1.0, although, because of inflation, it is usually greater than 1.0.

detection A past-oriented strategy that attempts to identify unacceptable output after it has been produced and then separate it from the good output (see also *prevention*).

distribution A way of describing the output of a common-cause system of variation in which individual values are not predictable but in which the outcomes as a group form a pattern that can be described in terms of its location, spread, and shape; location is commonly expressed by the mean or average or by the median; spread is expressed in terms of the standard deviation or the range of a sample; shape involves many characteristics, such as symmetry and peakedness, but these are often summarised by using the name of a common distribution, such as the normal, binomial, or Poisson.

experiment A planned set of operations that lead to a corresponding set of observations.

experimental unit One item to which a single treatment is applied in one replication of the basic experiment.

index number Device for measuring proportionate changes or differences in simple or complex quantities relative to their 'base' magnitude; index numbers of a time series, the most common type, represent magnitudes in given periods as percentages of their value in a base period.

index number problem   Differences in movement of a quantity (price) index resulting from the use of different weight bases if there is a systematic relationship between relative changes in quantities sold and prices.

individual   A single unit or a single measurement of a characteristic.

interaction   If the effect of one factor is different at different levels of another factor, the two factors are said to interact or to have interaction.

interval or **class interval**   A division on a frequency histogram marked off by boundaries, and all possible measurements that can fall between those two boundaries.

level of a factor   The various values of a factor considered in an experiment are called levels.

location   The general concept for the typical values or central tendency of a distribution.

lower control limit (LCL)   The lower boundary above which points plotted on a control chart can vary without the need for correction or adjustment.

lower control limit for averages (LCL$_x$)   The lower boundary on an average control chart, above which the plotted points can vary without need for correction.

lower specification limit   The smallest acceptable part produced by a process or operation.

machine capability   The short-term ability of a machine to make a part to the specified dimension. Usually measured by comparing the specified dimension to the spread (6σ) of the dimension being produced by that machine.

main effect   The average effect of a factor is called the main effect of the factor.

mean   The average of values in a group of measurements.

median   The middle of a group of measurements, counting from the smallest to the largest.

midpoint   The point of an interval which is an equal distance between the boundaries of an interval. The midpoint is found by dividing the width of the interval in half and adding this value to the lower boundary.

morale management   On-going process of improving factors that affect employee productivity and quality.

motivation   Motivational strength to satisfy a need.

np-chart   A type of attribute control chart that helps monitor the number of defective pieces in a production run.

non-comparative experiment   An experiment whose objective is the determine of the properties or characteristics of a population.

non-conforming units   Units that do not conform to a specification or other inspection standard; sometimes called discrepant or defective units; p and np control charts are used to analyse systems producing non-conforming units.

normal distribution curve   A type of curve in which the measurements tend to cluster around the middle. Because this curve is shaped like a bell, it is sometimes called the bell-shaped curve.

outcome (response-dependent variable)   Result of a trial with a given treatment is called a response.

out of control   A condition in which the points plotted on a control chart go outside the control limits. This condition indicates that an assignable cause is at work distrusting the process.

outgoing quality system   A system that uses statistical tools to determine whether or not the job is running satisfactorily and is producing parts that consistently meet the customers specifications.

Pareto analysis Helps set priorities on which problems to solve first, by sorting out the few really important problems from the more numerous but less important ones.

Pareto diagram A simple tool for problem solving that involves ranking all potential problem areas or sources of variation according to their contribution to cost or to total variation; typically, a few causes account for most of the cost (or variation), so problem-solving efforts are best prioritised to concentrate on the 'vital few' causes, temporarily ignoring the 'trivial many'.

percent defective p-chart A special type of attribute control chart. This p-chart shows the percentages of units that are defective or do not conform to specifications.

Poisson distribution Discrete probability distribution for attributes data: applies to non-conformities and underlies the c and u control charts.

precision A measurement's precision is related to its repeatability in terms of the deviation of a group of observations from a mean value. The terms 'accuracy' and 'precision' are often used interchangeably, but they may be distinguished: accuracy is the measure of the approach to a true value, and precision a measure of consistency or repeatability.

prevention A future-oriented strategy that improves quality and productivity by directing analysis and action towards correcting the process itself; consistent with a philosophy of never-ending improvement.

problem solving Process of moving from symptoms to causes (special or common) to actions that improve performance; among the techniques that can be.

process Combination of people, equipment, materials, methods, and environment that produce output – a given product or service; can involve any aspect of a business; a key tool for managing processes is statistical process control.

process average Location of the distribution of measured values of a particular process characteristic, usually designated as an overall average $\bar{X}$.

process control A state whereby statistical inference techniques are used to monitor and control a specified process in order to achieve improved quality and gains in productivity.

process control system A feedback mechanism that provides information about process characteristic and variables, process performance, action on the process, inputs, transformation process, and action on the output.

process spread The width of the curve formed by the frequency distribution. When compared to the specifications, the process spread tells whether the process can make parts within the specifications. Also written as 6σ.

production The process of transforming resources (inputs) into products (output) that satisfy human wants; sometimes used as a synonym for output, which is the result of the production process.

production and service improvement techniques (PASIT) The on-going process that involves organised use of commonsense to find easier and better ways of performing work and streamlining the production and service processes to ensure that goods and services are offered at minimum overall cost.

production worker The Bureau of Labor Statistics definition includes workers (up to and including the working foreman level) engaged in fabricating, processing, assembling, inspecting, receiving, storing, handling, packing and warehousing, shipping (but not delivering), maintaining, and repairing, as well as caretaker work, security services, product development, auxiliary production for the plant's own use, record-keeping, and other services closely associated with these production operations.

productivity (capital) The ration of total output to capital input.

productivity (computer operating expenses)   The ratio of total output to computer operating expenses input.

production (data processing expenses)   The ratio of total output to data processing expenses input.

productivity (labour)   The ratio of total output to labour input.

productivity (energy)   The ratio of total output to energy input.

productivity (materials)   The ratio of total output to materials input.

productivity (other administrative expenses)   The ratio of total output to other administrative expenses input.

productivity (partial)   The ratio of total output to one class of input.

productivity and quality challenges   Several issues that deserve significant attention while attempting to improve productivity and quality.

productivity and quality connection   Integrated relationship between productivity and quality.

productivity and quality coordinator   Company official charged with the responsibility of coordinating productivity and quality improvement programme.

productivity and quality evaluation and control   Evaluating the productivity and quality indicators of an organisation, task, plant, etc.

productivity and quality indicator   A factor, issue, or indicator that impacts on productivity and quality.

productivity and quality management   Integrated process involving both management and employees with the ultimate goal of managing the design, development, production, transfer, and use of the various types of products or services in both the work environment and marketplace; requires total involvement of everyone in the planning, measurement, evaluation, control, and improvement of productivity and quality at the source of production or service centre.

productivity and quality management checklist   A comprehensive self-assessment instrument for identifying areas of weaknesses that deserve productivity and quality improvement in an organisation.

productivity and quality management programme   A programme designed specifically to improve productivity and quality within an organisation.

productivity and quality management triangle (PQMT)   A formalised process of productivity and quality measurement, planning and analysis, evaluation and control, improvement and monitoring.

productivity and quality measurement   The process of measuring the productivity and quality at different levels such as at the task level, organisational level, or national level.

productivity and quality planning   Planning both productivity and quality variables within an organisation, task, plant, etc.

productivity and quality problems   Several factors affecting productivity level and growth rate and the quality of goods and services.

productivity (robotics operating expenses)   The ratio of total output to robotics operating expenses input.

productivity (total)   The ratio of total output to all input factors.

productivity (total factor)   The ratio of total output to the sum of associated labour and capital factor inputs.

productivity   The product of an effective and efficient productivity and quality management programme.

profitability analysis The explanation of changes in profits in terms of changes in total productivity and in 'priced recovery', defined as the ratio of prices received for outputs to prices paid for inputs.

quality Defined as 'fitness for use' by Juran; 'conformance to specification' by Crosby; 'fitness for use in terms of the ability to process and produce with less rework, less scrap, minimal downtime and high productivity' by Edosomwan.

quality characteristics Elements of fitness to use that typify the variety of uses of a given product.

quality circle (QC) A small voluntary group of coworkers from a plant or office who meet periodically to formulate and solve problems and thus raise productivity; in Japan, where this approach has been highly developed, the circle members are given special training in various problem-solving techniques.

quality cost (appraisal) Costs resulting from the extra effort expended to assure conformance to quality standards and performance specifications.

quality costs (external) Costs generated by defective products shipped to customers.

quality cost (internal) Cost associated with defective products and discovered prior to product delivery to the customer.

quality cost (prevention) Costs resulting from the prevention of non-conformance items.

quality costs Various categories of costs that are associated with identifying, avoiding, producing, maintaining and repairing products that do not meet specifications.

quality error removal (QER) technique Provides a framework, principles, and guidelines to a group of employees who voluntarily work together to select and solve key problem(s) affecting an organisation's work unit or task; organisational goals are broken down into small tasks at the operational level, and continuous effort is applied to improve productivity and quality within each work unit.

randomness Condition in which individual values are not predictable, although they may come from a definable distribution.

range Difference between the highest and lowest values in a subgroup; the expected range increases both with sample size and with the standard deviation.

repeatability Describes measurement variation obtained when one person measures the same dimension or characteristic several times with the same gauge or test equipment (sometimes referred to as 'equipment variation').

reproducibility A term popularised in the automotive industry as representing the variation in measurement averages when more than one person measures the same dimension or characteristic using the same measuring instrument.

response The numerical result of a trial based on a given treatment combination.

run A consecutive number of points consistently increasing or decreasing, or above or below the central line; can be evidence of the existence of special causes of variation.

run chart Simple graphic representation of characteristics of a process showing plotted values of some statistics gathered from the process (often individual values) and a central line (often the median of the values), which can be analysed for runs.

sample Several, but not all, of the possible measurements in a group of one kind of item.

shape General concept for the overall pattern formed by a distribution of values.

sigma (σ) Greek letter used to designate a standard deviation.

special cause   Source of variation that is intermittent, unpredictable, and unstable; sometimes called an assignable cause; signalled by a point beyond the control limits or a run of other non-random pattern of points within the control limits.

specification   Engineering requirement for judging the acceptability of a particular characteristic, a specification is never to be confused with a control limit.

sporadic problem   A type of problem that happens only once in a while.

spread   General concept for the extent to which values in a distribution differ from one another.

stability (for control charts)   The absence of special causes of variation; the property of being in statistical control.

stability (for gauge studies)   Variation in the measurement averages when the measuring instrument values are recorded over a specific time interval.

stable process   A process that is in statistical control.

standard deviation   A measure of the spread of the process output or the spread of a sampling statistic form the process (of subgroup averages); denoted by the Greek letter σ (sigma).

statistics   A value calculated from or based upon sample data (a subgroup average or range), used to make inferences about the process that produced the output from which the sample came.

statistical control   Condition describing a process from which all special causes of variation have been eliminated and only common causes remain; evidenced on a control chart by the absence of points beyond the control limits and by the absence of non-random patterns or trends within the control limits.

statistical process control   Use of statistical techniques, such as control charts, to analyse a process or its output to take appropriate actions to achieve and maintain a state of statistical control and to improve the process capability.

subgroup   One or more events or measurement used to analyse the performance of a process. Rational subgroups are usually chosen so that the variation represented within each subgroup is as small as feasible for the process (representing the variation from common causes), and so that any changes in the process performance (special causes) will appear as differences between subgroups; rational subgroups are typically made up of consecutive pieces, although random samples are sometimes used.

task-oriented total productivity measurement (TOTPM) model   A model for measuring the total productivity of a task and the organisation as a whole.

treatment combination   A set of levels of all factors included in a trial in an experiment is called a treatment or treatment combination.

type I error   Rejecting an assumption that is true; taking action appropriate for a special cause when in fact the process has not changed; overcontrol.

type II error   Failing to reject an assumption that is false; not taking appropriate action when in fact the process is affected by special causes; undercontrol.

upper control limit (UCL)   The upper boundary below which points plotted on a control chart can vary without the need for change or correction.

upper control limit for averages   The upper boundary on an average control chart, below which the plotted points can vary without need for correction.

upper specification limit   The largest acceptable part produced by a process or operation.

variable chart   A type of chart on which things or characteristics are plotted that are measured in numbers. The average and range chart is an example.

variable data   Data that come from things that can be measured. The measurements will vary from one piece to the next.

variation   Inevitable differences among individual outputs of a process; the sources of variation can be grouped into two major classes: common causes and special causes.

weight   Indicator of relative importance, such as prices, by which physical units of outputs or of inputs are combined to provide aggregate measures.

weight base   Period from which relative weights are drawn; may or may not be the same as the 'comparison base' from which values are set equal to 100.0 for index number construction.

worker participation   Approach to overcoming resistance to change through employee involvement in the planning and implementation of the change.

working condition improvement   A technique that involves a detailed audit of working conditions at each operation, designing improved working conditions, and installing and maintaining improvements in the working conditions.

work measurements   A means of determining an equitable relationship between the quantity of work performed and the number of labour hours required for completing the quantity of work.

work simplification   Systematic investigation and analysis of contemplated and present work systems and methods for the purpose of developing easier, quicker, less fatiguing, and more economical ways of providing high-quality goods and services.

zero defects   A quality philosophy that strives for virtually error-free production of goods and services.

25/2
.16
23ʃ

£24·50

L. Webb